STRATEGIC STUDIES INSTITUTE

The Strategic Studies Institute (SSI) is part of the U.S. Army War College and is the strategic-level study agent for issues related to national security and military strategy with emphasis on geostrategic analysis.

The mission of SSI is to use independent analysis to conduct strategic studies that develop policy recommendations on:

- Strategy, planning, and policy for joint and combined employment of military forces;

- Regional strategic appraisals;

- The nature of land warfare;

- Matters affecting the Army's future;

- The concepts, philosophy, and theory of strategy; and,

- Other issues of importance to the leadership of the Army.

Studies produced by civilian and military analysts concern topics having strategic implications for the Army, the Department of Defense, and the larger national security community.

In addition to its studies, SSI publishes special reports on topics of special or immediate interest. These include edited proceedings of conferences and topically oriented roundtables, expanded trip reports, and quick-reaction responses to senior Army leaders.

The Institute provides a valuable analytical capability within the Army to address strategic and other issues in support of Army participation in national security policy formulation.

Strategic Studies Institute
and
U.S. Army War College Press

THE ROLE OF LEADERSHIP
IN TRANSITIONAL STATES:
THE CASES OF LEBANON, ISRAEL-PALESTINE

Dr. Anastasia Filippidou
Editor

November 2014

*****

*****

Comments pertaining to this report are invited and should be forwarded to: Director, Strategic Studies Institute and U.S. Army War College Press, U.S. Army War College, 47 Ashburn Drive, Carlisle, PA 17013-5010.

*****

This manuscript was funded by the U.S. Army War College External Research Associates Program. Information on this program is available on our website, *www.StrategicStudies Institute.army.mil*, at the Opportunities tab.

*****

*****

The Strategic Studies Institute and U.S. Army War College Press publishes a monthly email newsletter to update the national security community on the research of our analysts, recent and forthcoming publications, and upcoming conferences sponsored by the Institute. Each newsletter also provides a strategic commentary by one of our research analysts. If you are interested in receiving this newsletter, please subscribe on the SSI website at *www.StrategicStudiesInstitute.army.mil/newsletter*.

CONTENTS

Foreword vii

1. Introduction 1
   Anastasia Filippidou

Part I: Conceptualizing Asymmetric
Leadership in Transitional Processes 15

2. Typologies of Leadership: Levels of
   Leadership and Approaches to Transition 17
   Anastasia Filippidou

3. Characteristics of Asymmetric
   Leadership 43
   Anastasia Filippidou

4. Asymmetric Leadership and
   Transitional Processes 71
   Anastasia Filippidou

Part II: Leadership in Volatile and
Transitional Situations Case Studies 83

5. The Case of Lebanon 85
   Elias Hanna

6. The Case of the Israelis
   and Palestinians 141
   Eyal Pascovich

Part III: Conclusions and Recommendations.....169

7. Conclusion and Recommendations 171
   Anastasia Filippidou

About the Contributors 197

FOREWORD

The United States plays a significant role in the Middle East. When dealing with the region, often the dilemma is: should there be a strong or weak regional leadership in order to facilitate a transitional phase? However, this decision is contextual, and a state must know what is its own foreign policy. To promote its national interests in the long term, the United States might have to prioritize the local interests and almost altruistically help the regions overcome their internal divisions and problems.

In this book, Dr. Anastasia Filippidou reviews the main leadership theories in order to set the foundations for analysis of asymmetric leadership in transitional processes. The report also examines the different leadership types and highlights that, with the exception possibly of toxic leadership, it is difficult, if not impossible, to determine that a specific type is better than another in every situation. According to Dr. Filippidou, some leadership styles are likely to be more effective in certain situations, and that a really effective leader is one who is able to determine the context of the situation and use the most effective leadership behavior required at the time.

The concept of asymmetric leadership is based on the notion that, when political leaders find themselves in a position which compromises their intents, which is often the case during transition, they adapt and adjust to the new realities not necessarily because they accept the causes for change, but because they need and want to survive. Leaders in transitional processes can find themselves in situations that compromise their intentions, which is often dictated by broader political circumstances and changes in the political environment. This idea of a constantly changing environment and its consequences validate the concept of asymmetric leadership. Dr. Filippidou conducts a review of leadership theory in Chapter 2 in order to establish a foundation for this study. Chapter 3 examines the phenomenon and key elements of asymmetric leadership and Chapter 4 examines the role of this leadership in transition processes. Part II of this work provides the case studies of Lebanon and Israel-Palestine, testing the theories discussed in Part I. In light of the unpredictable and always changing nature of asymmetric and survivalist leadership, understandably multiple challenges arise for those who have to face and deal with such leadership. Consequently, the Conclusion refers to specific recommendations for U.S. foreign policy decisionmakers in the Middle East.

DOUGLAS C. LOVELACE, JR.
Director
Strategic Studies Institute and
    U.S. Army War College Press

CHAPTER 1

INTRODUCTION

Anastasia Filippidou

BACKGROUND AND RESEARCH SYNOPSIS

The field of leadership studies is multidisciplinary, and inevitably there is a plethora of leadership definitions.[1] As a subject, leadership is very complex because it involves many different factors: the leader, followers, society, and even the pace of change. Admittedly, none of these facets will be the same in any given scenario, thus leadership is a dynamic process, which is complicated to confine within one specific and succinct definition. As this book demonstrates, even though situations and personalities can be too complex to have one size fits all, still human nature and leadership have certain transcending common elements allowing to draw lessons that can be transferable and applicable to various situations. As J. Blondel argues:

> If one reduces politics to its bare bones, to what is most visible to most citizens, it is the national political leaders, both at home and abroad, that remain once everything else has been erased; they are the most universal, the most recognized, the most talked about elements of political life.[2]

According to Marcha Geaney, there are so many definitions that the word is becoming meaningless,[3] while Peter Northouse compares defining leadership with the challenge of defining peace, love and democracy.[4] R. M. Stogdill argues that "there are almost as many different definitions of leadership as there are persons who have attempted to define the concept," while James MacGregor Burns poignantly states that "leadership is one of the most observed and least understood phenomena on earth."[5]

Northouse identifies four components as central to defining leadership: a process, influence, a group context, and entails goal attainment.[6] Leadership, Northouse argues, is a process whereby an individual influences a group of individuals to achieve a common goal. G. Yukl, after reviewing various theories reaches the conclusion that any definition of "leadership is arbitrary and subjective, and it depends, to a great extent, on the purpose of the researcher."[7] R. Bolden identifies two fundamental difficulties in defining leadership: firstly, leadership is an open concept based on subjective interpretation and secondly, it is based on the author's theoretical stance.[8] The latter consists of the trait and process approaches. The trait approach suggests that there are specific inborn or innate qualities or characteristics that make leaders, while the process approach suggests that leadership is behavior that can be learned by everyone.[9] Scholars who believe in natural leadership often attribute the required capabilities to traits.

T. Peters and R. H. Waterman in *In Search of Excellence* suggest that leadership traits also include the ability to develop a shared mission and sense of common values.[10] However, as the research will show more often than not, owing to the constantly changing environment and the complexity and variety of elements involved in a transitional situation leadership is based on both traits and process, and leaders are both, born and made.

Studies have shown that intelligence, dominance, self-confidence, energy or action orientation and task-relevant knowledge coincide with effective leadership.[11] However, these studies demonstrate a generally weak relationship of these traits to leadership. What is more, traits' centered research focuses on positive traits with less emphasis on negative traits that also can contribute to the rise of individuals to leadership positions. In sum, traits are not all-encompassing and fail to tell the whole story. Organizational structures and circumstances can determine the capabilities and traits that are considered most valued and most desirable.

Scholars of leadership often focus on hierarchy and power defining leadership as a "relationship between people in which influence and power are unevenly distributed on a legitimate basis."[12] Burns, a political scientist, considers leadership as awakening convictions within a collective and giving common direction to the desires and aspirations of individual members, while an organization is a polity that is a body whose members share resources, needs, and communal feelings. The job of the leader is to promote unity, cohesion, order, and performance of the group as a whole. Leadership, Burns contends, is exercised when "persons with certain motives and purposes mobilize, in competition or conflict with others, institutional, political, psychological, and other resources so as to arouse, engage, and satisfy the motives of followers."[13] This conception of leadership downplays command structure and instead emphasizes a sharing of common cause between leaders and followers. This definition suits very well the main focus of the research on asymmetric leadership in transitional processes.

Often leadership definitions are linked to power, referring to Max Weber's results' approach according to which power, and with that leadership, is the ability to get someone to do something they would not otherwise have done.[14] As it can be observed from the above succinct overview of definitions, leadership is often examined from the individual perspective, and, as such, it gives the impression of being monodimensional. On the whole however, leaders have to be aware of the complexity and diversity of their environments, as leadership challenges "are shaped by the unique dynamics of specific operations."[15] Despite the definition difficulties and although leadership is never going to be an exact science, the social identity approach fits best with the definitional requirements of this book.[16] In general, a leader would be the most representative of a group's identity, and would symbolize the sharing characteristics within the group and at the same time the differences with the opposing groups. Within this context, A. Haslam posits that "leaders embody a social identity that is shared with other group members [and] leaders exercise influence on this basis."[17]

FOCUS OF THE RESEARCH

Leadership is not static; it is a continuous process and ever-changing relationship between a number of different factors. Leadership style can be defined as "the patterns of behavior — words and actions — of the leader as perceived by others.[18] In this sense, it is very important how followers feel when leaders attempt to influence them. The research focuses on political leadership in transitional and volatile situations and the efforts and the role of leadership in the transformation process from weak and fragmented states or communities to peaceful and viable states. The research is not based on a specific model of leadership and definition, but a combination of models, because the thesis of the research is that leadership, and especially asymmetric leadership, is too complex to be based on just one model. To paraphrase Laurence Peter, "some problems are so complex that you have to be highly intelligent and well informed just to be undecided about them."[19] As described already in this book, many of the types of leadership just overlap. After all, "out of the crooked timber of humanity no straight thing was ever made."[20]

The current research reviews the characteristics and elements expected of effective leadership of radical political movements (asymmetric leadership) within an ever-changing and complex environment. The emphasis of this work is not so much on psychological attributes, but on the incentive structure and institutional and contextual constraints for leaders, because good governance matters for good leaders and not only vice versa. It is nearly impossible to develop a universal checklist for leadership. The focus of this research is on asymmetric leadership in transitional environments. However, the research aims to demonstrate the necessity for a constant balancing of different characteristics of leadership and adjustment of leadership styles to continuously changing situations. By focusing on leadership, this book isolates, and at the same time highlights, one of the key determining elements which affect and influence a political transition from conflict to peace and normalization. The objectives of the research are to provide answers to questions such as: What are the main leadership challenges in transitional environments, and how do leaders cope with them? What is the role of asymmetric leadership in transitional processes? Which skills and characteristics are necessary for successful leadership in transitional processes?

RESEARCH DEFINITIONS

Scholarly debate focuses on whether the difference between successful and great leadership depends entirely on the situation.[21] Partly, this holds true as, for instance, it is fairly certain that Winston Churchill would not have been considered great without World War II. As the current analysis focuses on leadership in transitional states and processes, it is worth clarifying, then, at this stage that the research predominantly refers to effective or successful leadership, and not to great leadership. Asymmetric leadership of radical political movements operates within an environment of uncertainty and risk as part of daily operations from a position of weakness compared to conventional leadership. As it will be examined in the following chapters, especially in Chapter 3, the survivability of this type of leadership relies on flexibility and adaptability to the situation and the environment. Transitional states or transitional processes refer to the transformation process from weak and fragmented states or communities toward a peace process leading to peaceful and viable states. When referring to transition in this research, it can be twofold: the transition of the country and/or the transition of leadership.

WHY ASYMMETRIC POLITICAL LEADERSHIP IN TRANSITIONAL STATES

Political leadership denotes the ability "to make others do a number of things (positively or negatively) that they would not or at least might not have done."[22] Leadership has a very significant role in transitional processes, given the ability of the leader to shape and define the future of a country and its structures. S. A. Renshon identifies three characteristics highlighting the importance of political leadership: decision centrality, the extension of public sphere responsibilities, and the structural amplification of effects.[23] Decision centrality suggests that it is simply impossible to hold a public vote on every political issue; even in a democracy, more often than not leaders take decisions without any direct input from the electorate. The second characteristic — the extension of responsibilities — is directly relational to the leaders' decisionmaking role. The structural amplification of the effect of leaders' decisions is evident in the proliferation of government agencies and organizations charged with the implementation of a leader's decisions. The ability of leaders to shape the emerging structures is enhanced by the changing character of the period, which makes it important to understand how the different actors operate under such conditions.

The top-driven nature of political transitional processes, combined with the associated uncertainty, signifies that leaders are crucial in shaping the process. Thus it is essential to focus on political leaders — radical or not — during transitional periods, examining successes and failures in moving the regime toward a peace process. As discussed with reference to the survivability of leaders, a transitional leader has to engage in creative destruction and reforming and rebuilding institutions and practices at the same time.[24]

Despite the definitional difficulties outlined earlier, the phenomenon of leadership has been studied universally since ancient times. Sun Tzu reflected upon the responsibilities of political and military leaders as custodians of the states well-being, and he cautioned on the activities of leaders that were beneficial or detrimental to the state. Confucius, Plato, and Aristotle are among the philosophers who have written on leadership. Plato classified political leadership into *timocratic* leadership, which is ruling by pride and honor (*timi* means honor); Plutocratic leadership, signifying ruling by wealth and prosperity (*plutos* means wealth); Democratic leadership (ruling by popular consent); and tyrannical leadership, which is ruling by authoritarianism and oppression.[25] In the 1800s, Thomas Carlyle advocated:

> universal history, the history of what man has accomplished in this world, is at bottom, the history of the Great Men, these great ones; the modelers, patterns, and in a wide sense creators of whatsoever the general mass of men contrived to do or to attain.[26]

Ever since, the belief that leaders were born with the gift of leadership prevailed. Emergence theories sought to explain leadership in terms of traits (Traits Theories), and people who believed in traits tend to explain the fortunes of humankind on the basis of individual contributions and acts. In this sense, history developed as it did because of the actions of "great men." Following this, the concept of leadership was examined from the functional and situational perspectives.[27] Adair's functional approach seeks to bring the qualitative and situational approaches to leadership within the realm of the interaction of task, team, and individuals' consideration. Therefore, leadership by creating the aim, planning for and encouraging the group, is able to accomplish the aim.[28] The above were followed by theories that focused on the interaction between leaders and followers (servant leadership and charismatic leadership theories), while other theories focused on leaders and their interaction with the environment (contingency and transformational theories).[29] Leadership is a borrowed and dependent identity; a leader needs followers in order to be a leader.

Certain scholars of organizations have been dismissive of leadership, as they argue that factors such as structure and culture determine much, if not most, individual action. Thus rules, regulations, and structure restrict those in leadership position as much as they govern the lowest subordinate. This dismissal of leadership represents a reaction to the overemphasis on the "great man" theories in the past, as scholars often attributed mankind's great achievements to great individuals. Even though organizations may deal with routine matters most of the time, but crises demand leadership. Furthermore, something very fundamental in human nature makes people desire to be leaders. Leadership is also important for organizations because of the conflicts and issues it may raise. Thus leadership will always remain an important issue. Revolutions, coups, and takeovers are, more often than not, contests and conflicts over leadership.

A transitional process is one of instability and uncertainty, as key actors seek to determine their positions within the new structures and rules. Most transitions in the end take place or are finalized at the top, with a relatively small number of people making final decisions. Furthermore, the initialization, at least of the implementation phase, also takes place at the top. There can be, of course, and there are, bottom-up mass movements initiating change, and there can be contacts at grassroot level initiating or pressuring for peace processes, but still at some point there is top-down decisionmaking at strategic leadership level to legitimize the transitional process. In this sense, either in a bottom-up or a top-down led process, the onus lies with the political leadership to formalize a transitional agreement.

Leadership, as well as conflict transformation and resolution, share common traits, such as relationship building and inclusiveness. Leadership is only one of the elements for conflict transformation and transition, but it impinges directly onto the other various transformations, such as structural transformations. However, leadership can also be part of the problem either on a personal or on a group level. On a personal level, because the predominant role of a leader might be his own survival and not the resolution of a conflict and a transition to peace; and on a group level, because the conditions, real or perceived, may not be seen as ripe for a favorable resolution and transition.

RESEARCH STRUCTURE

This book examines the role of asymmetric leadership in transitional states. Part I provides a brief review of leadership theory. Chapter 2 establishes a foundation for this analysis. When assessing the ability of asymmetric political leadership to shape an emerging system, it is essential to consider personal attributes, the environment, and the character of the regime.[30] These combined elements determine the extent to which leaders are able to influence and shape events. Personal characteristics of political leaders refer to the ability to inspire followers. For instance, for a leader possessing charisma, faults and errors may be ignored or trivialized by followers, which reduces barriers to the exercise of power.[31] According to G. Pasquino, during transition, political leaders have to transfer their authority to organizational structures and compete under the new rules to remain effective[32] and to remain in power. Therefore, Chapter 2 focuses on typologies of leadership. Chapter 3 examines the phenomenon and key elements of asymmetric leadership, and Chapter 4 examines the role of this leadership in transition processes. Part II of this book provides the case studies — Lebanon and Israel-Palestine — that test the theories discussed in Part I.

ENDNOTES - CHAPTER 1

1. See, for instance, John Adair's Action-Centered Leadership Model, Victoria, UK: Gower Publishing, 1979; and John P. Kotter, *Leading Change*, Watertown, MA: Harvard Business Review Press, 2012; Peter Northouse, *Theory and Practice*, Thousand Oaks, CA: Sage Publications, 2010.

2. J. Blondel, *Political Leadership: Towards a General Analysis*, London, UK: Sage Publications, 1987, p. 1.

3. Marcha Geaney, "Appreciative Inquiry and Relational Leadership," presented at the New Jersey Organization Development Conference, May 2005.

4. Peter Northouse, *Leadership — Theory and Practice*, Thousand Oaks, CA: Sage Publications, 2010.

5. R. M. Stogdill, *Handbook of Leadership: A Survey of the Literature*, New York, Free Press, 1974, p. 259; and James MacGregor Burns, *Leadership*, New York: Harper and Row, 1978, p. 18. See also M. Rejai and Phillips Kay, *Leaders and Leadership: An Appraisal of Theory and Research*, Westport, CT: Praeger Publishers, 1997, p. 1.

6. Northouse, *Leadership*, pp. 3-4.

7. G. Yukl, *Leadership in Organizations*, Upper Saddle River, NJ: Pearson Prentice Hall, 2006, p. 8.

8. R. Bolden, "What Is Leadership Development: Purpose and Practice?" Leadership South West Research Report, Binghamton, UK: Centre for Leadership Studies, 2005, available from *business-school.exeter.ac.uk/research/areas/centres/cls/research/publications/abstract/index.php?id=66*.

9. Northouse, *Leadership – Theory and Practice*.

10. T. Peters and R. H. Waterman, *In Search of Excellence*, New York: Random House, 1982.

11. Stogdill.

12. J. L. Bowditch and A. F. Buono, *A Primer on Organizational Behavior*, New York: John Wiley & Sons, 1994.

13. Burns, p. 18.

14. W. J. Mommsen, *The Political and Social Theory of Max Weber: Collected Essays*, Chicago, IL: University of Chicago Press, 1992.

15. L. Forster, "Coalition Leadership Imperatives," *Military Review*, November-December 2000, pp. 55-60, especially p. 56.

16. H. Tajfel and J. C. Turner, "An Integrative Theory of Intergroup Conflict," W. G. Austin and S. Worchel, eds., *The Social Psychology of Intergroup Relations*, Monterey, CA: Brooks/Cole, 1979, pp. 33-47.

17. A. Haslam, ed., *The New Psychology of Leadership: Identity, Influence and Power*, New York: Psychology Press, 2011.

18. P. Hersey, *The Situational Leader*, Escondido, CA: Center for Leadership Studies, 2004, p. 25.

19. Laurence Peter, *The Peter Principle: Why Things Always Go Wrong*, New York: HarperCollins Publisher, 2009.

20. I. Kant, "Idea of a Universal History on a Cosmo-Political Plan," *The London Magazine*, pp. 385-393.

21. J. Antonakis, A. Gianciolo, and R. Sterberg, *The Nature of Leadership*, London, UK: Sage Publications, 2004, Chaps. 7 and 12.

22. Blondel, pp. 2-3.

23. S. A. Renshon, "Political Leadership as Social Capital: Governing in a Divided National Culture," *Political Psychology*, Vol. 21, No. 1, 2000, p. 202.

24. G. Breslauer, *Gorbachev and Yeltsin as Leaders*, New York: Cambridge University Press, 2002.

25. Plato, Πολιτεία *(Republic)*.

26. Thomas Carlyle, *On Heroes, Hero Worship and the Heroic in History*, London, UK: Echo Library 2007, p. 1.

27. Adair, Action-Centered Leadership Model.

28. John Adair, *Training for Leadership*, London, UK: Macdonald and Co, 1970, pp. 15-22.

29. Burns, pp. 19-20; and B. M. Bass, *A New Paradigm of Leadership: An Inquiry into Transformational Leadership*, Washington, DC: U.S. Army Institute of the Behavioral and Social Sciences, 1996.

30. Blondel, p. 28.

31. B. Kellerman, "Leadership as a Political Act," Kellerman, ed., *Leadership: Multidisciplinary Perspectives*, Upper Saddle River, NJ: Prentice Hall, pp. 63- 89, especially p. 83.

32. G. Pasquino, "Political Leadership in Southern Europe: Research Problems," *West European Politics*, Vol. 13, No. 4, 1990, pp. 118-130.

PART I:

CONCEPTUALIZING ASYMMETRIC
LEADERSHIP IN TRANSITIONAL PROCESSES

CHAPTER 2

TYPOLOGIES OF LEADERSHIP: LEVELS OF LEADERSHIP AND APPROACHES TO TRANSITION

Anastasia Filippidou

The study of leadership has received increased attention with theories ranging from the more classical leadership theories associated with traits and hereditary qualities, to the more recent examination of social identity approaches. Leadership is a broad theme with numerous associated theories branching out from the main original theories, and there remains considerable debate vis-à-vis which ones remain relevant today. This chapter provides an overview of different types and frameworks of leadership, and it emphasizes the diversity of qualities and traits that enable a person to become a leader. The examination of the phenomenon of leadership can be dated back thousands of years, with views on what makes good leaders being used to inform the selection of leaders and predict their behavior. In the ancient Greek world, Socrates identified a list of leadership skills, emphasized the importance of knowledge and examined the idea of leadership being situational. Also, Xenophon, a contemporary and admirer of Socrates, focused on strategic leadership and risk and emphasized the importance of leading by example.

Leadership can be divided into three levels: top leadership with very high visibility, middle-level leadership including leaders from different sectors, and grassroots leadership consisting of local community leaders and local organizations. In a conflict resolution process for instance, top leadership focuses on high level politics and high profile negotiations; middle level leadership focuses on training in conflict resolution, peace commissions and problem-solving workshops; while grassroots leadership puts its emphasis on local peace committees, work in post-conflict trauma and prejudice reduction.[1] In the 16th century, according to Niccolo Machiavelli, a leader needed a mix of ruthlessness, cynicism, and amorality to gain and then to hold onto power.[2] In the 19th century, Carl von Clausewitz stressed the importance of moral forces in the commander to overcome friction: will power, resolution, and intelligence.[3] According to Clausewitz, leaders must be able to exercise sound judgment, despite the lack of certainty, if objectives are to be achieved.

TYPES OF LEADERSHIP

Leaders select their methods based on both personal and organizational needs and aims. Circumstances, organizational structure, and history are among the elements that determine the degree and type of leadership needed. K. Grint presents a four-fold typology of leadership definition: position (where leaders operate that makes them leaders), person (who leaders are that makes them leaders), result (what leaders achieve that makes them leaders), and process (how leaders get things done that makes them leaders).[4] O. Kroeger identifies four key elements of leadership that are common to many definitions and theories: First, leadership is about using power, and effective leaders are able to access their individual power at the right time to get the desired result; second, the means by which leaders decide to use their power involves judgment; third, leadership involves using power intentionally against a specified aim; and fourth, leadership involves interactions between people.[5]

In view of the fact that leadership is a people-centered activity, it follows that the personalities of the people affect how they access their power, make judgments, and carry out leadership. However, when dealing with human nature and especially people in crises and transitions, typologies can be too clinical and often become redundant, as the boundaries of the various types and approaches are transcended. For instance, the emphasis on a specific type may depend on the duration of a conflict. Therefore, a result-based approach may be more important in a short-term conflict and transition process, while, during a protracted conflict, the focus may be on the process. According to F. Fielder, leaders are either task- or relationship-oriented, but the effectiveness of orientation depends on the situation.[6] For Fielder, in an unfavorable situation, the group is expected to be told what to do without consultation, and task-oriented leadership works best. In moderate situations, however, where leaders have moderate power and support in combination with a complex task, consultation is necessary to achieve followers' buy-in, and, in this case, relationship leadership is most suitable.

Leadership occurs in many forms, but ultimately culminates in two competences: selecting the best option among alternative courses of action, as well as bringing and keeping followers on board. What is more, typology matters more for those who, for whatever reason, need and want to examine the different types of leadership rather than for the followers. More often than not, the emphasis is on rational aspects of leadership and on whether leaders achieve their promises, while not enough emphasis is laid on the emotional aspects of leading. In this sense, even though it might seem irrational for some to follow a specific leader, others interpret and receive words and nonverbal communication differently and become followers.

LEADERSHIP THEORY OVERVIEW

A prevailing theory in the 19th century is the "great man theory" (GMT), according to which leadership is inherent. In other words, according to GMT, leaders are born and not made. This theory seems to have certain references to contingency theory (CT), as the belief was that great leaders would come to the fore when faced with the fitting situation. Originally, this was predominantly linked to upper class and educated men. While today this theory is no longer just limited to men or to class, the "born or made" debate remains the focus of research and writing.[7]

Although trait theory (TT) could be traced back to 380 BC, the theory resurfaced in the 1930s through psychologists like Gordon Allport who argued that people are either born with or develop qualities that enable them to shine as leaders. TT focused on analyzing mental, physical, and social characteristics in order to form a better understanding of the combination of qualities required for effective leadership. However, these studies were inconclusive, with little consensus on the essential elements required of leaders. Allport, for instance, identified almost 18,000 English personality-related terms.[8] Still, even though TT fell off grace, discussion came back to specific qualities and traits demonstrated by successful leaders. TT seems to be making a comeback reinforced by advances in genetics.[9]

According to the Five Factor Leadership Trait theory, "significant relationships exist between leadership and individual traits such as: intelligence, adjustment, extraversion, conscientiousness, openness to experience general self-efficacy."[10] Trait approaches dominated decades of scientific leadership research. However, more recently these approaches were criticized for what was seen as an inability to offer a clear distinction between leaders and nonleaders and "for their failure to account for situational variance in leadership behaviour."[11] S. J. Zaccaro argues that combinations of traits and attributes integrated in conceptually meaningful ways are more likely to predict leadership than additive and independent contributions of several single traits.[12] The trait approach fails to take into consideration patterns or integrations of multiple attributes. Furthermore, this approach does not distinguish between those leader attributes that are generally not malleable over time and those that are shaped by, and bound to, situational influences. Additionally, the trait approach fails to consider how stable leader attributes account for the behavioral diversity necessary for effective leadership.[13] Consequently, in contrast to the traditional approach, the leadership attribute pattern approach is based on theorists' arguments that the influence of individual characteristics on outcomes is best understood by considering the person as an integrated totality rather than a summation of individual variables.[14] The inclusive nature of the attribute approach does not discount any aspects that may have influenced the creation of personality traits and the person.

In the early-1940s, TT led on to the development of Behavioral Theories (BT), which obviously laid emphasis on the behavior of effective and ineffective leaders rather than their characteristics. BT divided leaders into task-focused and people-focused and concluded that leaders are made and not born. Using authoritarian, democratic, and *laissez-faire* leadership styles as a basis for this work, it was concluded that some leaders were more people-oriented, while others were more task-oriented. It soon became clear that leader effectiveness is contingent on interplay of factors relating to both the leader and the situation.[15] In the 1960s, CT argued that the specific leadership styles were only suited to particular situations, and that a leader's effectiveness depended on how well the leader's style fit the context.[16] As such, leaders could perform very well in certain circumstances but very poorly in others. According to John Adair, the performance of a leader depends on the situation, and he attempted to provide a framework to match leaders to situations. Adair's action-centered approach is an example of CT. Adair argues that the team, the task, and the individual needs must all be taken into account, and therefore leadership is a result of what you do and not what you are.[17] Still, what you do is also behavioral, and therefore it is affected in some way by what you are. One of Adair's shortcomings is that he assumes that one size fits all.

As mentioned earlier, no single leadership style can be right for every leader under all circumstances and in all situations. Consequently, situational theories (ST) were developed to highlight that leadership depends upon organization, task, leader-follower relationship, and other environmental factors. ST developed alongside CT. Situational leadership places primary importance on the tasks and challenges facing the organization itself rather than the personal traits of the leader, and it proposes that leaders must be able to adapt their leadership style as the situation changes.[18] Linking this to R. Tannenbaum and W. Schmidt's "Continuum of Leadership" made this theory very popular.[19] Transitional processes with constantly changing circumstances call for constant adaptability and adjustability of leaders, which, as discussed in Chapter 3, is not always possible. In this sense, leaders' capabilities have to match the organization's immediate needs, that is, its constantly changing situation. As the situation changes, leaders have to adjust and adapt constantly if they want to maintain power. According to P. Hersey and K. Blanchard, situational leadership theory recognizes the existence of multiple variables in leadership, and, as such, leaders could not possibly hope to cope with this high level of complexity. Consequently, leaders have to prioritize and focus on the relationship between leader and followers, because, as mentioned before, without followers, all other variables will be irrelevant. Thus leaders must adjust their styles according to the situation presented. Hersey and Blanchard identify four different leadership styles associated with task and relationship behavior: selling, telling, delegating, and participating.[20] The different styles depend on the situation, the relationship behavior (amount of support needed), and task behavior (amount of guidance needed). See Figure 2-1.

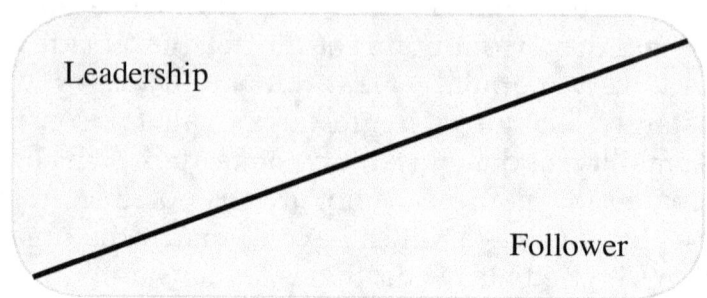

Autocratic Protective Participative Delegating Anarchic

Figure 2-1. Leadership-Followers
Relationship and Related Leadership Styles.

Following Hersey's and Blanchard's logic, a leader's behavior has to be adjusted to that of the followers.[21] Robert House argues that the leader's task is to make smooth the followers' path to the shared goal by removing barriers and by facilitating motivation, and that the leader's behavior should match the requirements of the followers and the situational characteristics.[22] As such, the leader has to select the appropriate style to smooth the followers' path to the goals. Therefore, according to House, ambiguous tasks require directive leadership in order to reduce uncertainty and to increase the probability of the outcome; dangerous situations require supportive leadership in order to increase self-confidence and encourage followers; participative leadership is required when transition has advanced and when followers are ready for empowerment; and, result-oriented leadership is suitable when followers have high result-orientations.[23]

One of the strengths of situational leadership is that it can provide leaders with a set of different styles they can use, depending on the situation. Given the complexity of transitional processes and the variation of reasons to follow a leader at times, and for some of the followers the leader will need to implement different leadership styles depending on the circumstances and the followers. See Figure 2-2.

DUE TO COPYRIGHT RESTRICTIONS
SOME OR ALL IMAGES ARE NOT INCLUDED

Figure 2-2. Diagram adapted from Hersey, 2004.[24]

Leadership styles, as well as readiness levels, are situational, and the leadership style should correspond to the readiness level of the follower. Based on Figure 2-2, the leadership style (S1-S4) has to correspond to the readiness level (R1-R4). In order for the leader-follower relationship to be effective, the leaders have to be aware of the followers' readiness, and the latter should be aware of the leaders' wants and needs. Leaders, for instance, based on the readiness and behavior of the followers might have to adjust their leadership style to influence the followers' behavior, while followers, based on the leader's needs, might have to adapt their behavior to implement leaders' requests and demands.

As mentioned in the introduction one of the roles of leadership is, through a rational and emotional appeal depending on the issue and the followership, to unite "our side" and differentiate us from the others. Benedict Anderson refers to this as the "imagined communities."[25] According to Anderson, as we could never really meet everybody from "our side" and as such we could not really know whether other people are really like us, we simply could imagine that this was the case or not.

Transactional and Transformational.

Leadership models can help explain what makes leaders act in a specific way. Within this context, E. P. Hollander developed the concept of transactional leadership,[26] while Burns in the late-1970s introduced transformational leadership theories.[27] Transactional leaders take people as they are, motivating through their existing needs and goals. With transactional leadership, followers are motivated by exchange or transaction of something of value leaders possess or something that is within their authority to grant to followers. Thus, transactional leaders and followers exchange something of value the leader possesses or controls that the followers want in return for their services.

The type of power transactional leaders adopt depends not only on the followers and their needs, but also on the personality of the leader and the kind of power they are able to use. Transactional leaders are characterized by the leaders' relative separation from their followers. Transactional leadership can involve mutual influence, but, given the unequal dynamic of the relationship between leaders and followers, the leader retains more power than the followers and tends to base that power more on reward and coercion and less on interpersonal and influencing skills.

Consequently, the aims by these leaders may simply reflect their personal views of the organization's needs or transactional leaders may simply pursue their own objectives utilizing the organization as a means. As mentioned earlier, these types of leaders motivate followers to implement their decisions through reward, coercion, threat, intimidation, and the application of imperative force. Hence, transactional leaders prefer to create order, search for cause and effect relationship and predictability, and they value control.[28] In radical political organizations, transactional leaders face limits to the degree and efficacy of their actions. Coercive power is based on raw power but in radical political movements, membership more often than not is voluntary, thus it is difficult to sustain commitment through the leader's constant use of raw power over the followers.

On the whole, Transactional Theory, also known as Exchange Theory (ET), focused on the human desire to maximize benefits and minimize costs to the individual, and argues that a leader must reward, or not punish success, to get the best out of the followers. As such, leaders have to try and synchronize individual and organizational goals. Transactional leadership as a long-term approach seems impossible in the leadership environment this research focuses on because if morale, discipline, ideology, commitment, and comradeship are based on a simple value, transaction can endanger success. Nevertheless, transactional leadership may be necessary in protracted critical situations when followers might lose their motivation and when command and obedience become even more vital. The risk of transformational leadership is that leaders could misuse the motivation and confidence for their own goals and for self-preservation. Transformational leaders may seek to transform, but what happens if the organization does not need transforming or if the organization does not need the transformation the leaders wants.

At times, leaders may decline leading by avoiding responsibility for key decisions, such as choosing the future direction of the organization or resolving a crisis. This avoidance of responsibility may be due to a leader's will for self-preservation or incapability. The subject of leader survivability is analyzed more in depth in the following sections.

As a normative approach to leadership, transformational leadership looks beyond the existing system, and aims to offer goals and objectives to followers. Transformational leadership takes the process beyond holding and using power. According to Burns, "leaders induce followers to act for certain goals that represent the values and the motivations—the wants and needs, the aspirations and expectations—of both leaders and followers."[29] Under this type of leadership, the emphasis is not on the leader but instead on the perception of those being led. Organizations in transitional processes have to be prepared to perform different tasks influenced by factors over which they have no control. Under these circumstances, individuals are expected to adapt continuously in order to function in new environments. It is the responsibility of the leaders to have the organization prepared to be able to adjust according to the task. This calls for transformational leadership which must have the ability to realign the organization with unforeseen and unexpected situational changes so that they can achieve the task. A radical political organization is an amalgamation of a number of groups in need of constant realignment and adjustment. Transformational leadership requires a different attitude from that associated with task accomplishment. One of the core components of transformational leadership is seen to be charisma, as the leader inspires trust and respect, which are used to encourage desired behaviors. Transformational leaders seek to raise the level of human conduct and ethical aspiration of both the leader and those he leads, and thus it has a transforming effect on both, trying to connect leaders and followers with a common sense, understanding and vision.[30]

As such, transformational leaders empower their followers, increase their levels of morality and motivation, and encourage mutual support. Transformational leaders inspire followers through charismatic leadership, trust, a sense of belonging, and shared ownership of the goals. Within this context, B. M. Bass asserted that transformational leadership is of a higher order than transactional leadership, and that it "originates in the personal values and beliefs of the leader, not in the mutually dependent exchange of leader and followers."[31] Transformational leaders are inspired by the perceived needs and wants of the people they lead. In turn, followers are inspired by these leaders. A leader would take carefully calculated risks and try things. After all, "it is easier to get forgiveness than permission." Transformational leaders provide or facilitate the creation of a new vision for the followers and create a sense of shared purpose and obligations. As such, transformational leadership brings leaders and followers closer and reaches further into the follower's international motivation. The division of leadership styles into transactional and transformational considers leadership either as a means of exchange or to "shape and alter and elevate the motives and values and goals of followers."[32] However, both types of leadership have their role in volatile transitional processes. Given the variety of membership in political organizations and the constantly changing circumstances, a leader at times will use transactional and at other times transformational leadership.

Over the past 20 years, there has been significant research on toxic leadership. While opinions diverge on the specific traits and skills associated with toxic leaders, there seems to be a wide consensus that these leaders work toward self-promotion at the expense of the group. Toxic leaders can be successful in the short-term, but in the end, they leave the organization in a worse state than they found it, often with long-lasting damage to the culture of the organization and the psychology of the individuals within the group. During transitional processes with increased polarization and constant change, the conditions may be fertile for toxic leaders to come to the fore. However, their rise is often circumstantial, and their success is usually short-lived, and it does not translate into the equivalent success during the normalization phase. After all, it is the very short-term success that often protects a toxic leader.

Visionary and Inspirational: A Trait and a Style(?)

G. C. Avery examines transformational leadership within a paradigm of "emotion in leadership" which allows her to categorize it under visionary leadership. Much like inspirational leadership, the main idea is that the leader's ability to make emotional connections and create visions to inspire followers to greater achievements. Interestingly, Avery observes that the transformational or visionary leaders depend more on followers, rather than themselves, to implement the vision.[33] What is more, most leaders in hierarchical organizations that utilize transformational leadership will, at any one time, be both leader and follower and therefore require skills to carry out both roles. Consequently, effective leaders must ensure that they understand not only themselves, but also their followers below them as well as their superiors above them. Paraphrasing Bill George, inspirational leaders would have to have a very good understanding of the purpose, history and vision (knowledge), have strong values (behavior), establish trusting relationships (connectedness), act on their values and demonstrate self-discipline (consistency), and believe strongly in the mission and transition process (passion).[34] A strength of inspirational leadership style is that it helps leaders to understand their own strengths and weaknesses, to create a trusting relationship with their followers, while it also seems to include some of the best qualities of transformational leadership.

According to A. Haslam, the theories discussed earlier are too individualistic, and he categorizes them as the "old psychology of leadership." He describes them as a perspective, portraying leaders as inflexible, nonpredictive, and qualitatively lacking.[35] Haslam argues that it is not about leaders, but about followers; it is not about me, but about us, and it is not about power over, but rather power through. Consequently, he proposes Social Identity Theory (SIT) based originally on Henri Tajfel and John Turner's work in the 1970s and 1980s as a better prism of examining leadership. SIT focuses on explaining intergroup behavior and relationships in order to investigate the phenomenon of leadership. For Haslam, there are four key elements to leadership: being one of us; doing it for us; craft a sense of us; and make us matter. At the core of his thesis is that leaders exert influence based on the shared social identity of the organization.[36]

Example, Persuasion, and Compulsion.

As mentioned earlier, there is a plethora of leadership models. However, Figure 2-3 illustrates the most and least effective elements for short- and long-term successful political leadership.

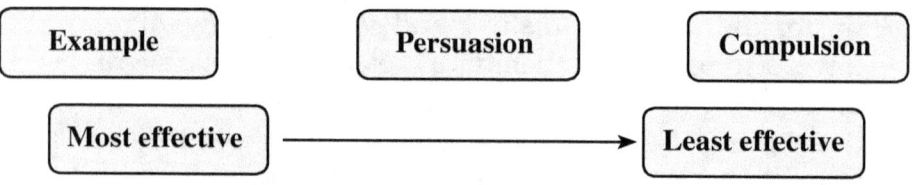

Figure 2-3. Leadership Models.

Starting from the left of the figure, leading by example in both the short and long term can be ideal but not always realistic, given for instance the need for continuity and hence the protection of the leader. From the follower's perspective, leading by example signifies agreement with the leader and his actions. When leadership employs persuasion, that still constitutes effective leadership as in the end it achieves consensus to a common cause. Owing to the unequal dynamic of the relationship between leaders and followers, leaders may demand and obtain compliance from their subordinates and followers, but this compliance can never be guaranteed unless followers are persuaded and buy into a process. As Robert Greenleaf posits, leadership by persuasion has the virtue of change by convincement rather than coercion, with obvious advantages.[37] With persuasion, leaders appeal both to the interests and the emotions of followers. Although Carlyle's leaders are meant to solve the problems of their subordinates, through persuasion leadership is related to making followers face up to their own responsibilities and become stakeholders in the transition process. The complexity of transition processes often demands leaders to be able to ask the right kind of questions, which also entails the involvement of the followers in order to find a commonly accepted solution. In this way, the authority and decisionmaking responsibility is shared between the leadership and followers, because often in complex situations only a collective engagement can address the challenges and fully exploit the opportunities of the transition process. The leader is somebody who does not feel the burden of what Z. Bauman calls the "unbearable silence of responsibility."[38]

A need for compulsion signifies lack of cohesion within an organization and, although imposing one's will on followers can be effective initially, it will be ineffective and ineffectual in the long term, prohibiting any successful transition to a peaceful and stable state. In sum, leading by example would represent the purest and most effective form of leadership; appealing to emotions and persuading followers can yield positive results; while compulsion, if at all effective in the leadership type examined in this work, could only be in the short term. The optimum would be for a leader to be egalitarian enough to generate contentment among followers, but at the same time to be authoritarian enough to generate efficiency among followers. Certain distancing between leaders and followers appears to be common-place, irrespective of the country and the cultural background. Empirical observations show that proximate leaders are more efficient and more successful than distant leaders. In

33

contrast, Niccolo Machiavelli supports that distance is a useful device to prevent followers from noticing the weaknesses of leaders.[39] Leaders have to maintain a specific persona within the organization and with the opponents if they are to establish a god-like presence. Consequently, getting the distance right is critical in order to maintain the mystique of leadership. Nowadays, maintaining this social distance and air of leadership mystery, even for clandestine organizations, is much more difficult with the continuous media reporting. This leadership style is discussed further in later sections.

A. Etzioni distinguishes three types of compliance: coercive, calculative, and normative.[40] Crises and complicated and protracted problems are associated with normative compliance. Understandably in a transitional process, which is a complex and complicated problem, a leadership cannot force people to follow them. It is the very nature of the problem with its consequences that requires followers to want to participate in transitional processes. Followers have to want to give their time and, on occasion, even their lives to achieve a political party's or a movement's goals. Pragmatically, given the complexity of a transitional process and the variation within a followership at different times, in different situations, and on different followers, all three types of Etzioni's compliance would be used. Still, the optimum would be for a leadership to achieve collaborative compliance.

Culture and Leadership.

The chapter has already highlighted the importance of context vis-à-vis leadership, and at the epicentre of context is culture and cultural differences.[41] According to Mary Douglas, culture can be captured based on two criteria: grid and group.[42] Grid refers to the significance of roles and rules in a culture, which can be either rigid or loose. Group refers to the importance of the group in culture. Some cultures are highly group oriented, while others are more individual oriented. For Douglas, when a culture represents both high grid and high group, there tends to be rigid hierarchies, such as in clandestine organizations in which the "cause" and the group are more important than the individual. "When a leader establishes a goal with the troops," advocates Sun Tzu, "he is like one who climbs to a high place and then tosses away the ladder" because if followers feel threatened but can see an escape route (the ladder), they may take it.[43]

However, if there is no escape, then the followers will have to commit themselves to a fight for survival and, as Sun Tzu suggests, "put them in a spot where they have no place to go, and they will die before fleeing."[44] This is when followers' survival and goals become one, and followers fully commit to the cause. One of leadership's trait is empathy, with the ability to step into another's shoes. Empathy is a requirement to address protracted and complex problems because, if a leader cannot understand how the followers see the problem, how could a leader mobilize followers? When culture remains high group but low grid and lacks the concern for rules and roles, there is egalitarianism where consensus in decisionmaking is vital. If there is both low group and low grid, there are individualist cultures for whom the collective or rules is perceived as unnecessary. Last, if there is low group and high grid, the isolated individuals can see themselves undermined by the power of rules and roles. In sum, hierarchists consider rules and power critical; egalitarians prioritize greater solidarity; individualists lay emphasis on greater freedom; while fatalists just give up.

With the exception of the last option which is quite fatalistic, throughout a transitional process, all three options of hierarchical, egalitarian, and individualist will be employed. Here again, a leadership would have to achieve a balance and avoid the paradox where a political leader in a crisis needs the consensus of the followership, but also owing to the complexity of the problem, there cannot be an open and inclusive decisionmaking process. Grint stresses the interconnectedness between egalitarians, hierarchists, and individualists, and that egalitarians are limited by an endless search for consensus for a solution. However, Grint argues that, because of this paralysis of decisionmaking, there is a need for hierarchists in order to be able to reach decisions and also individualists in order to protect individuals.[45] As such, political leadership in transitional processes needs to strike a balance between high grid and high group without undermining the leadership itself. The rhetoric of a political leadership, in order to make a cause attractive, can be egalitarian but in reality, the leadership remains highly hierarchical. After all, as mentioned earlier, even though collaborative compliance should yield the best results in transitional states, even egalitarian leadership would still require somebody to take the lead; otherwise, the leaders will be considered as irresponsible and incompetent.

As situations change, leaders with different leadership styles are needed. At times, leaders can be proscriptive and have a style that emphasizes giving explicit instruction and setting specific aims. Other leaders can be collaborative and delegate decisionmaking to subordinates, presenting them with aims and allowing them to select their own means of achieving these aims. However, in radical political organizations the stakes can be very high in combination with the clandestine *opus operandi* of these organizations. Even though the leadership might appear to be collaborative on the surface and that they listen to the followers and subordinates, in reality, they are very proscriptive organizations claiming to act in the name of the community or group of people they claim to represent. This is another aspect where asymmetric leadership in transitional situations has to strive for a balance between proscriptive and collaborative styles. By being proscriptive, the leadership ensures that the subordinates and followers remain on board, while by being collaborative, leaders aim to achieve and maintain legitimacy. On the one hand, in radical political movements, the leadership has to be proscriptive because it cannot risk independent thinking and acting within its ranks. But on the other, the leadership has to be collaborative because its membership is based, by and large, on voluntary compliance, as the members do not really **have** to be, they **chose** to be part of a radical political organization. So under these circumstances, a leadership would not want uncommitted or disgruntled followership. After all, despite the different types of leadership, by nature, leadership entails inequality. As N. Harter argues, this in-egalitarianism is both legitimate and necessary, but this inequality is mutually beneficial to leaders and followers with the proviso that certain safeguards are being maintained.[46]

Even though this chapter makes clear that there appears to be a total lack of consensus on what constitutes an effective leader, there seems to be a growing acceptance that each theory has something to offer in terms of developing understanding of what elements could be inherent or developed in good leaders. Chapter 3 brings together the theories discussed in this chapter, in combination with the specific characteristics of asymmetric leadership. Figure 2-4 depicts the evolution of leadership theory.

The Evolution of Leadership Theory

*This is not surpring, as Myrdal has pointed out, that a concern for leadership is a distinctly American phenomenon, R.M. Stogdill, *Individual Behaviour and Group Achievement*, New York: Oxford University Press, 1969, p. 3.

DUE TO COPYRIGHT RESTRICTIONS
SOME OR ALL IMAGES ARE NOT INCLUDED

Source: B. S. C. Watters, *Leadership in Defence*, Shrivenham, UK: The Defence Leadership Centre. Ministry of Defense, 2004.

Figure 2-4. Leadership Theory: A Chronology.

ENDNOTES - CHAPTER 2

1. J. P. Lederach, *The Moral Imagination: The Art and Soul of Building Peace*, Oxford, UK: Oxford University Press, 2005.

2. N. Machiavelli, *The Prince* (Penguin Classics), New York: Penguin Books, 1961.

3. Carl von Clausewitz, M. Howard, ed. and trans., *On War*, Princeton, NJ: Princeton University Press, 1984.

4. K. Grint, *Leadership: Limits and Possibilities*, London, UK: Palgrave/Macmillan, 2005.

5. O. Kroeger, J. M. Thuesen, and H. Rutledge, *Type Talk at Work*, New York: Dell Publishing, 2002, p. 66.

6. F. Fielder, *A Theory of Leadership Effectiveness*, New York: McGraw-Hill, 1967.

7. John Adair, *Great Leaders*, Guildford, United Kingdom (UK): The Talbot Adair Press, 1989, pp. 37-38.

8. G. W. Allpot, *The Nature of Prejudice*, New York: Perseus Books Publishing, 1979. Also see G. Matthews, I. J. Deary, and M. C. Whiteman, *Personality Traits*, 2nd Ed., Cambridge, UK: Cambridge University Press, 2003, p. 3.

9. D. Day and J. Antonakis, *The Nature of Leadership*, Thousand Oaks, CA: Sage Publications, 2012, pp. 7-8, and Chap. 16.

10. J.A. Smith and R. J. Foti, "A Pattern Approach to the Study of leader Emergence," *The Leadership Quarterly*, Vol. 9, pp. 147-160.

11. S. J. Zaccaro, "Trait-Based Perspectives of Leadership," *American Psychologist*, Vol. 62, No. 1, January 2007, pp. 6-16.

12. *Ibid.*

13. *Ibid.*

14. *Ibid.*

15. V. L. Reardin, "Predicting Leadership Behaviours from Personality as Measured by the Myers-Briggs Type Indicator," Dissertation, Raleigh, NC: North Carolina State University, 1996, p. 50.

16. R. G. Funnel, *Leadership – Theory and Practice,* Seares House Papers, 1981, p. 137.

17. John Adair, *Leadership Skills,* London, UK: IPD, 1997, p. 11.

18. F. E. Fiedler, *A Theory of Leadership Effectiveness,* New York: McGraw-Hill, 1967.

19. R. Tannenbaum, W. H. Schmidt, "How to Choose a Leadership Pattern," *Harvard Business Review,* May-June 1973, pp. 162-175, reprint of the original HBR article of March–April 1958.

20. P. Hersey and K. H Blanchard, *The Management of Organizational Behavior,* Upper Saddle River, NJ: Prentice Hall, 1977.

21. *Ibid.*

22. Robert J. House, "A Path-Goal Theory of Leader Effectiveness," *Administrative Science Quarterly,* Vol. 16, 1971, pp. 321-338.

23. *Ibid.*

24. P. Hersey, *The Situational Leader,* Escondido, CA: Centre for Leadership Studies, 2004.

25. B. Anderson, *Imagined Communities,* New York: Verso, 1991.

26. E. P. Hollander, "The Essential Interdependence of Leadership and Followership," *Current Directions in Psychological Science,* Vol. 1, No. 2, April 1992, pp. 71-75.

27. James MacGregor Burns, *Leadership,* New York: Harper and Row, 1978.

28. A. C. Gayle, *Understanding Leadership*, London, UK: Sage Publications, 2004, p. 144.

29. James MacGregor Burns, *Leadership*, New York: Harper and Row, 1978, pp. 19-20.

30. *Ibid.*, p. 20.

31. B. M. Bass, *A New Paradigm of Leadership: An Inquiry into Transformational Leadership*, Washington, DC: U.S. Army Institute of the Behavioral and Social Sciences, 1996, p. 5.

32. Burns, p. 425.

33. G. C. Avery, *Understanding Leadership*, London, UK: Sage Publications, 2004.

34. P. Northouse, *Leadership – Theory and Practice*, Thousand Oaks, CA: Sage Publications, 2010, pp. 208-211.

35. A. Haslam, ed., *The New Psychology of Leadership: Identity, Influence and Power*, New York: Psychology Press, 2011.

36. *Ibid.*

37. R. Greenleaf, *Servant Leadership: A Journey into the Nature of Legitimate Power and Greatness*, Mahwah, NJ: Paulist Press, 2002.

38. Z. Bauman, *Postmodern Ethics*, Oxford, UK: Blackwell, 1993.

39. Machiavelli.

40. A. Etzioni, *Modern Organizations*, London, UK: Prentice Hall, 1964.

41. See, for instance, C. C. Chen and Y. T. Lee, *Leadership and Management in China*, Cambridge, UK: Cambridge University Press, 2008; and A. S. Tsui, S. S. Nifadkar, and A. Ou, "Cross-National Cross-Cultural Organizational Behavior Research," *Journal of Management*, Vol. 33, No. 3, 2007, pp. 462-468.

42. Mary Douglas, *Natural Symbols*, London, UK: Routledge, 2003; and Mary Douglas, *Purity and Danger*, London, UK: Routledge, 2008.

43. Sun Tzu, *The Art of War (Nine Grounds)*, Oxford, UK: Capstone Publishing, 2010.

44. *Ibid.*

45. Grint.

46. N. Harter, F. J. Ziolkowski, and S. Wyatt, "Leadership and Inequality," *Leadership*, Vol. 2, No. 3, 2006, pp. 75-94.

CHAPTER 3

CHARACTERISTICS OF ASYMMETRIC LEADERSHIP

Anastasia Filippidou

Hyper-turbulent, hyper-accelerating conditions increasingly typify the organization world of the 21st century, according to Kim S. Cameron and Robert E. Quinn.[1] They label it "adhocracy culture" and one that is dynamic and creative. This type of culture closely aligns to that of a radical political organization in a transitional process, which is constantly facing new circumstances. It also requires changes in rigid structures and involves innovative and adaptable thinking in leadership. In addition, Cameron and Quinn contend that this adhocracy leadership style requires vision, innovation, and an ability to take risk. This supports the thesis of this book that a changing situation—the transitional process—requires a combination of leadership styles and, as such, requires adaptable leadership. Thus the optimum leader would be somebody with an ability to understand context and lead change through necessary communications' methodologies.

Context, as mentioned in Chapter 2, is important as it defines the broader social and political sphere in which the leader has to operate. Contextual constraints range from custom and previous practice through to institutions, which can introduce restrictions as well as opportunities.[2] One of the main arguments of this book is that the most important factors that distinguish effective leaders often lie outside the control of an individual leader. Although leaders must have the ability to exploit the opportunities offered by external factors, irrespective of how good they may be, leaders cannot really guarantee effectiveness by their own actions. However, there are external factors that allow a leader to be recognized as successful, in addition to individual attributes required of the individual to make the most of the opportunity presented. See Figure 3-1.

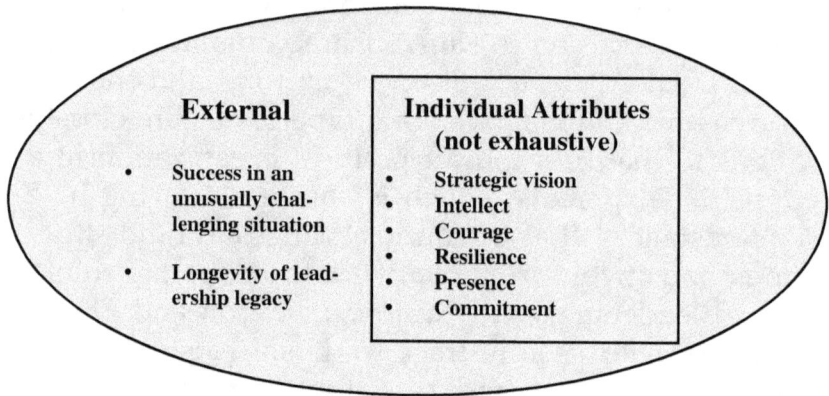

Figure 3-1. External Factors for a Leader to Be Recognized as Successful; Individual Attributes Required to Make the Most of a Presented Opportunity.

As argued already, asymmetric leadership is complicated and complex, and it is critical at all levels and within organizations that need to make decisions that "address longer time spans of responsibility, that are faced with more complex situations, and are faced with dealing with environment relationships."[3] This argument is supported since violent political organizations are both complex in their organization and the manner in which they deliver output. In this sense, political leadership is viewed as "a process of influencing people to accomplish the mission, inspiring their commitment, and improving the organization."[4] To paraphrase Stephen Rosen, violent political organizations are unique organizations that, owing to their very nature, promote and reward from within.[5] The advancement of followers and subordinates could therefore be subjective if the weighting given by the assessing leader to loyalty and adherence to orders is deemed more important to the organization than the application of acquired knowledge to yield better results.

For a leader to remain at the top over a period of time during conflict and through transition to normalization requires constant adaptability and self-awareness, as advocated by the Situational Leadership Theories. As already discussed, asymmetric leadership in transitional and volatile situations in order to survive is adaptable and moves between the different leadership styles, such as from transactional to transformational, depending on the specific circumstances. For leaders of political organizations, the ideology underpinning the organizations provides a solid basis from which to exercise transformational leadership that can be achieved through numerous interactions. At the same time, the grip on the organization can be accentuated and reinforced through a more transactional style, based on an uncompromising approach to discipline and procedure. This is not because leaders do not know what they want, but because they know they have to adapt the means to achieve their ends. This is a logical and pragmatic approach, given the security risks of direct contact with other members of the political organization; but without direct contact, it is difficult for leaders to provide transformational leadership.

More often than not, a combination of leadership styles is needed in asymmetric leadership in order to steer the organization from the different phases of conflict toward peace processes. Throughout this transition, effective leaders have to be able at times to lower the expectations of the very organizations they are leading so as to reach a deal with the other side. At times, they have to fulfill the demands and needs of their followers in order to secure the continued buying in of the followers in the transitional process. Furthermore, the dealings of leaders with those external to the organization they are leading are initially predominantly transactional as they seek to maximize the benefits and minimize the costs of transition to their organizations.

It is only when there is a realization that a transitional process and the way out from a protracted conflict has to be inclusive involving a compromise of all the conflicting sides, that leadership shifts from transactional to transformational. In this sense, leaders acknowledge that they need their own side, as well as the opposing side, to agree to come to the table and reach a commonly accepted agreement. Within this context, leaders need to inspire transformation of their own people, as well as that of the opponents, and help build Sun Tzu's golden bridge. Few, if any, leaders will conform to only one leadership model. Still, as mentioned earlier, this does not make theories redundant. Indeed, the applicability of a number of theories to individual leaders facilitates a deeper understanding of the individual and therefore the conceptual understanding of leadership.

The main elements of asymmetric leadership are flexibility and adaptability. Inevitably, during transitional processes, asymmetric leadership is constantly changing, both internally (within the organization itself) and externally (within the state). The elements of flexibility and adaptability are not meant in the sense of leaders not knowing the pathway and course of the organization. Instead, flexibility and adaptability is meant as a necessary means to achieve ends. As such, asymmetric leadership has to be rigid enough so as to set its direction and destination, and flexible enough to be able to reach that destination. Asymmetric leadership has to accept that it competes in an environment of uncertainty and risk as part of ordinary daily operations. Thus flexibility is key in asymmetric leadership. Owing to this flexibility and adaptability, asymmetric leadership is able to change course as new opportunities emerge quicker than more conventional types of leadership.

Leaders help to create organizational cultures and then try to reinforce them through their communication with followers and their actions. Therefore, asymmetric leadership can be symbolic but also more directly involved in the day-to-day operations of the organization, where the leader is seen as an active decisionmaker instead of just a distant or formal authority figure. Within this context and under transitional circumstances, leaders encourage reasoned risk-taking down the hierarchy. Risk-taking in transitional processes is defined as taking calculated risks to resolve pressing operational problems as quickly as possible. The duty of followers is to try and understand and accept what the organization wants done, and then do it. This responsibility is reinforced by repeated encouragements and admonitions by the leader to focus on the end, notwithstanding the daily challenges. In this sense, members of radical political movements buy in to the needs and wants of the leadership and consequently it becomes a collective obligation to succeed.

With asymmetric leadership in political transitional processes, the focus is on creative problem-solving and reasoned risk-taking. As a result, the leadership anticipates and responds to environmental changes rapidly to capitalize on opportunities and manage problems and develops flexible operating policies. The risk acceptance in combination with flexibility in transitional processes denotes the need to find solutions and apply them quickly. Asymmetric leadership aims to take advantage of unstable environments through operational flexibility and acceptance of risk. After all, the very nature of a radical political organization is based on asymmetric culture where the norm is uncertainty and flexibility and the organization exists "on the edge."

To sum up, risk and uncertainty lead to a crisis, which in turn leads to an often opportunistic decision-making. Furthermore, for the members of the organization, if there is a challenge, there is an imperative for a response and an action in order to accomplish the task. This operational commitment of the members leads the above mentioned "buying in," and it leads to a "we and me" culture with high institutional, but at the same time high in-group, collectivism.

The we and me culture encourages commitment to and cooperation with both the political organization as a whole and their individual teams. Followers and members of radical political organizations are therefore encouraged to cooperate broadly through the we culture but also at the same time to take greater individual and team responsibility for outcomes through the me culture. Subsequently, followers were also encouraged to be both collectively and individually responsible for operational performance. Given the nature of asymmetric leadership — within the organization and outside it—in transitional processes, decisionmaking has to be quick. It is centralized for strategic decisions and at the same time decentralized for local operational decisions.

In view of the fact that membership in radical political organizations is predominantly voluntary, both actions and results are of high importance in order to retain membership and commitment to the cause. Success in asymmetric leadership becomes a "must succeed," with its reliance to voluntary membership and the belief in a cause instead of the "can succeed" of symmetric leadership with its reliance on established institutions and structures. In asymmetric leadership in transitional processes, there appears to be a stronger sense of urgency and assertiveness in achieving the objectives of the organization, while also more trust is placed in their fellow members of the organization and their leaders, rather than in systems.

As argued previously, the main elements of asymmetric leadership is flexibility and adaptability, but also unpredictability. The latter is understandably augmented during transitional processes. Radical political organizations with asymmetric leadership are by definition and intent, imbalanced or disjointed to some extent. Consequently, under these circumstances, a leader's role would be to anticipate and prepare members for the unexpected, instead of minimizing or systematizing it. Flexibility and dealing with the unexpected quickly and effectively represents advantages and opportunities instead of threats to the organization and its goals. A transitional process in itself entails uncertainty. In transitional processes, attitudes, behaviors, and values change over time, and the effectiveness of decisions may be judged by a different leader who may not hold the same values as the original decisionmaker. This can be positive and escalate commitment, or it can be negative and lead to goal disorientation for instance.

At the epicentre of asymmetric leadership is inspiration and vision in combination with the ability to grasp the nature and complexity of political transition. A vision in itself implies transition, and a move toward something more positive in the future. A vision challenges people to transcend the status quo and to commit themselves to worthwhile causes connected to the larger community. The implementation of a vision, however, would require the "buying in" from, and the voluntary compliance of, the followers as it will be them, in the end, who are going to implement this vision. Thus, as stated already under asymmetric leadership vision, strategies and goals come from the top, but facing local challenges are largely decentralized. In addition, asymmetric political leadership involves the capacity to overcome the different types of constraints that might be caused by domestic or external factors. Thus, as discussed already, asymmetric leadership combines different elements from different leadership types; on certain issues it is transformational, envisioning a better future for the followers and helping them get there, and on other issues, it is transactional in an effort to try and overcome constraints through the use of trade-offs.

As stated in the introduction, in asymmetric leadership in radical political movements, the leader-follower relationship is at the same time fluid and rigid. Leaders need to strive constantly to maintain favorable relations with their followership, and, consequently, they need to regularly negotiate new bases for collaboration. Simultaneously, the relationship has to be rigid enough to assure compliance and commitment to the cause of the organization. In transitional processes, there is a human cost if conflicts are not transformed successfully and quickly. Time is of the essence, and there is no liberty to spend the time required to build consensus on every detail, and a bias for action will be required. Therefore, during crises and transitional processes, there is not always time for inclusive discussions and therefore the circumstances legitimize coercion as necessary for the public good. On the other hand, leaders need the followers' to buy into the transitional process. Followers' compliance is secured through fear and threats and punishments followers would want to avoid. Coercive power is based on raw power, but in radical political movements, membership more often than not is voluntary. Consequently, it is difficult to sustain commitment through the leader's constant use of raw power over the followers.

INFORMAL TIES

Leadership is a phenomenon involving the leader, the followers, and the situation, and, as such, it is a constantly changing process. It is a relationship and an experience affecting one another in an interactive complex process rather than a linear one. As mentioned already, leadership is situational, and therefore it has to be examined within context, while it also impacts on the leader at a personal and aggregate level. Early leadership theories discuss specific traits leaders should have, such as initiative, intelligence, talkativeness, etc., but the importance of these traits depended on the context.[6]

Even organizations that function under strict rules and regulations still rely on informal social ties to achieve their tasks. Through these informal ties, networks are built, which are systems of personal ties maintained along-side formal structures and with all the benefits networks bring. In general, leaders of radical political organizations often emerge in primary groups consisting of people connected by informal social ties. These informal links enhance loyalty to the organization and the aims, while they also help with trust-building among the members of the organization. In consequence of these informal ties and because of the strong ideological links within the organizations under examination in this chapter, leaders are often socio-emotional. Socio-emotional refers to nonmaterial, though personally gratifying, communications and activities that are part of nearly every human group: personal validation, companionship, recreation and expressions of esteem.[7] In most radical political movements, individuals rise to the top who are particularly skilled and forthcoming in personal and emotional matters; individuals who are approached in a crisis for sympathy and understanding. These individuals are socio-emotional leaders and, in ideologically motivated organizations, these leaders are crucial. Socio-emotional rewards such as good feelings and personal affirmation promote adherence to role expectations and stability of structure.

One of the most important leadership activities is the promotion of stable and productive relationships within organizations. This is particularly true in complex organizations pursuing multiple goals and objectives. Radical political organizations are network-based organizations with complex structure, and the diversity of tasks can counteract factors leading to cohesiveness. The variety of responsibilities and objectives can lower members' visibility and importance to each other. In addition, the clandestine nature of such organizations makes face-to-face relationships almost impossible to maintain. These conditions can render coordination within the organization difficult, and the sense of common purpose upon which these organizations depend can be undermined. This can lead to the disintegration of the orgainzation, which is why relationship building is a vital role for leaders.

A generalized feeling that both followers and leaders will benefit eventually from their role in their organization can create a more stable system. In radical political organizations with asymmetric leadership, followers' participation in the organization is predominantly voluntary. Leaders and followers believe in a shared higher cause and as such the "buying in" from the followers' perspective is already present. As mentioned in Chapter 2, in radical political movements, the most effective leaders aim to develop mutual links of trust and voluntary collaboration with their followers. Effective asymmetric leadership aims to reduce perceived differences between their interests and aims and those of their followers. As Follet states, "one person should not give orders to another person, but both should agree to take their orders from the situation facing the organization."[8]

ASYMMETRIC LEADERSHIP, PARADOXES, AND MISCONCEPTIONS

There is the false belief of holding out for a hero. This is false because the supply of heroes is scarce and unreliable, while at the same time, it seems as if followers are aborting their own responsibilities, expecting a leader to do everything. What is more, during transitional periods, the luxury of time to hold out for a hero just does not exist. As Jean Lipman-Blumen states, most people view leaders through a distorted lens emphasizing their strengths and minimizing their failings.[9]

From this follows the utopian portrayal of a charismatic leader. Leaders with charisma are believed by their followers to have powers and abilities that exceed those of everyday individuals. Charisma can allow flaws to be overlooked, albeit this is temporary until there is failure to move toward a peace process and transition to normalization. This type of leadership is primarily defined by who the leaders are, and often this approach is based on an emotional relationship between leaders and subordinates. According to Émile Durkheim, followers actually want their leaders to be god-like in their powers.[10] In the original Greek, the meaning of hierarchy is "holy sovereignty." *Archi* means ruler or sovereignty, and *ieros* means divine. *Hierarchia* signifies a sacral ranking, and therefore the concept of hierarchy is the sacred organization space that facilitates a god-like leadership.

As mentioned earlier regarding the distance between leaders and followers, leadership has to be treated as sacred to maintain its legitimacy. The shortcomings of the god-like approach are that followers can make irrational choices and may render subordinates incapable of judging what is wrong and right. More precisely, the "Great Man" approach allows followers to abort decisionmaking responsibility to leaders, and, if the decision is proven wrong, the subordinates can blame their leadership.

For Max Weber, charismatic leadership can be differentiated between power and authority and distinguishes three different kinds of authority.[11] According to Weber, traditional authority occurred when subordinates followed because they had always done so; in rational-legal authority, it is rational for subordinates to follow; and in charismatic authority, leaders attract followers devoted to the leader's powers that seem to provide the possibility for a radical and previously unknown solution to some kind of social crisis. The last one, charismatic leadership, constitutes the only form of noncoercive authority, but because the charisma is embodied within an individual, it usually dies out with that individual or becomes routinized through an institution.[12]

Weber argues that charismatic leaders seek fundamental and radical changes in society, necessitating destruction of conventionally accepted practice. Like Niccolo Machiavelli, Weber's account of political leadership referred to those with a strong instinct for power.[13] Charismatic leaders appear to have supernatural qualities derived from powers outside themselves. Thus followers feel the duty to obey these leaders because of the higher forces from which their powers derive. For James MacGregor Burns, charismatic leaders are power-wielders, that is, leaders who safeguard loyalty and dedication from followers that satisfy the leaders' interests instead of the followers'.[14] Power-wielders maintain followers' obedience to an organization of ideals and not adherence to an ideal organization. Within this context, power-wielders tend to achieve high levels of dependency among their followers and, in effect, disempowering their followers.

To an extent, followers can share their leader's charisma by being members of the same group and organization. Furthermore, often people in desperate and volatile situations want to believe in the ability of the charismatic leader to help them and protect them in times of emergencies. Thus, charismatic leadership should still be acknowledged as an important force, even if it is not often encountered. Radical political organizations, because of the very nature of these organizations with their need for voluntary compliance and at times their demand for sacrifice on behalf of the followers, may be expected to breed charismatic leaders from time to time. In crises situations, charismatic leaders may prove vital in decisionmaking. However, when time comes to move on and progress to a different phase of transition, charismatic leaders often prove reluctant, to say the least, of handing power over to the successors. Thus, there appears to be a fundamental flaw in the general belief that leaders are indispensable. What is more, when charismatic leaders are gone, it is not always clear that their achievements can be sustained or that their very actions as charismatic individuals undermine the possibility of sustainable actions by the followers.

Also, what happens when crises do not exist? Charismatic leaders may be impelled to maintain crises if resolving would undermine their authority. Leo Tolstoy's criticism of the charismatic leader is very poignant when he likens this type of leaders to bow waves of moving boats, always in the front and in theory leading, but in reality just being pushed along by the boat itself. Interestingly, pragmatic and objective examination of the lives of charismatic leaders reveals them to be less mysterious than they might initially appear. What is more, the rise to charismatic leadership is not spontaneous, but takes planning, organization, and staging.

According to Burns, there are four types of transformational leaders: intellectual leaders, revolutionary leaders, heroes or ideologues, and leaders of reform.[15] As discussed in Chapter 2, the aim of transformational leadership is for the leader to transform people and followers into something better. As a result of this transformation, followers are prepared to be true to their better selves.[16]

A paradox is that, although people value their freedom, they also realize that collective activity requires leadership. Followers acknowledge that leadership is necessary for organizing a group of people, but, at the same time, followers do not like to surrender themselves any more than necessary. This paradox has often been a point of friction between leaders and followers, and it has led to discontent and distrust. As it has been argued throughout this book, leadership is dynamic and not static; in the same way, followership has to be proactive and not passive for the leader-follower relationship to be successful and flourishing. In this sense, followers have to be transformed from followers to active supporters of the leader and of the activities and policies.

ASYMMETRIC LEADERSHIP AND FOLLOWERSHIP

Leaders and followers are linked in relationships of mutual dependence. As stated already, leadership is a borrowed identity, and leaders cannot exist unless they induce others to implement their decisions. Since the focus is on the charismatic leader with the extraordinary nature, theorists shifted their focus on the relationship between leaders and followers which is based on deeply held and shared ideological values. Thus, charismatic leaders achieve unique goals through followers who are exceptionally loyal to, and deeply trusting of, their leaders. Under these circumstances, followers are willing to make personal sacrifices that might appear irrational to outsiders in the interest of the shared vision.

Crises, which are normal, allow limited time for decisionmaking and action-taking, which is often associated with authoritarianism. To his rhetorical question, "Whether it is better to be loved, or feared, or the reverse," Machiavelli clearly sides with fear, arguing that "it is far better to be feared than loved if you cannot be both. The Prince must nonetheless make himself feared in such a way that, if he is not loved, at least he escapes being hated."[17] Leaders, irrespective of how charismatic they might seem, are still human and, as such, flawed and imperfect. Often, in crises there is a need for decisionmakers who are perceived as god-like in their decisiveness and their ability to provide answers. However, in transitional situations and state building processes, which have to be inclusive and egalitarian processes in order to stand a chance of success, a god-like authoritarian leadership might prove counterproductive. What is more, god-like leaders more often than not end up fighting for their own survival and self-preservation as rulers rather than for the successful transition to peace. The need for self-preservation is examined in Chapter 4.

Leaders do not really enter into conflict contemplating failure. Failed leaders can become single minded and get involved in tactical decisions and lose objectivity. Hence they surround themselves with followers whose advice and opinion is limited to uncritical compliance and destructive consent (UCDC). In these cases, even when they know their leader is wrong, they feel they have reasons—self-preservation, new role within the organization, etc.—not to say anything, and therefore they consent to the damage of their own leader and possibly of their own organization, too. To this end, these leaders start seeking crises, as by maintaining an emergency status, they can maintain authority and their post. Leaders tend to legitimize their decisions and actions on the basis of a suitably persuasive account of the situation. Consequently, UCDC signifies another form of leader-follower dysfunction, as consistently uncritical followers allow their leader to detach themselves from reality, create their own and often self-serving reality, and develop delusions of grandeur and, as such, set either impossible or detrimental objectives for the organization.

Leaders have to be able to operate independently in an ambiguous, changing, dynamic, and politically sensitive environment. Accordingly, effective leaders are meant to surround themselves with people who complement their skills, and therefore leaders are advised to seek people who demonstrate intelligence, judgment, and the capacity to anticipate in support.[18] However, in reality political leaders are constrained in their ability to take into consideration advice from their followers as they are leading hierarchical organizations that are complex in their construct and their *modus operandi*. As mentioned earlier, leadership is a relationship, and Karl Popper suggests that it is the responsibility of followers to impede leaders' shortcomings and to remain constructive dissenters.[19] In this way, followers can help keep the organization on track and achieve its goals, thereby prohibiting leaders from undermining these. In effect, followers and leaders accept that neither is perfect, and all share responsibility. Once again, a balance is necessary between dedicated and independent followers to be responsible followers, and for a constructive relationship between leaders and subordinates. Leaders do not need to be perfect. Instead, they have to be aware of the limits of their knowledge, ability, and power, and that these limits can lead them to destruction unless they can rely on their followers to compensate for their own limits.

Although Carl Clausewitz viewed the commander's knowledge as an essential capability, current research shows that stand alone components and traits are not effective unless they are combined and coordinated. Leadership is much more complex than a linear relationship, with the leaders limited to just giving commands and exercising power and authority over the followers. In point of fact, in asymmetric leadership in transitional processes, the leader-follower relationship is very fluid, owing to the nature of the unequal dynamic, but at the same time, it is also a rigid relationship, because of the need for trust within the organization. Thus, leaders need to maintain favorable relations with their followership, but to achieve that, they need to negotiate regularly for new bases for collaboration. Usually organizations require leaders with traits, skills and characteristics that match their immediate needs. However, in radical political organizations, often the leader plays a significant role to the very formation of the organization and its needs.

Effective leadership requires consistent partnership between leaders and followers in a way that meets the needs and advances the aims of both. Leadership is a dependent, if not borrowed, identity in the sense that somebody is a leader because somebody else is a follower. Irrespective of the type of leadership, leaders and followers are linked in a relationship of mutual dependence. The **legitimation** of leaders depends on the relationship between the followers and the leaders. A person is a leader because there are followers. In point of fact, as Grint advocates, it is the followers who teach leadership to leaders, as it is not just experience that counts but reflective experience.[20] As he argues, learning is not so much an individual and cognitive event, but a collective and cultural process. In the words of S.

Kierkegaard, "life can only be understood backwards, but it must be lived forwards."[21] As explained in the introduction, the focus of the book is on asymmetric leadership, and where the association between followers and leaders becomes rigidly asymmetric in either direction, the relationship breaks down. This renders the success of an organization short-lived because feedback and learning is minimized.

THE ROLE OF POST-TENURE PROSPECTS FOR LEADERS: THE NEED FOR SURVIVABILITY

Maintaining the Status Quo.

Leaders on an individual level are often reluctant to admit the need for changes lest it be seen as weakness among both supporters and opponents. As such, leaders can fall victims to their own rhetoric and propaganda. During a conflict lasting for years, they can demonize the other side, but during the transition phase, they have to persuade their own, as well as the opposing side, that they can coexist peacefully in the future. Again, a leader would have to try to strike a balance between overselling and underselling a peace agreement. If they oversell an agreement, the leaders may cause frustration to the followers if goals and promises are not materialized during the implementation phase. But if they undersell the agreement, it will be difficult to persuade the followers to buy into the agreement, rendering its implementation difficult, if not impossible.

During a transition, political leaders have to deliver their own people and simultaneously reassure them that the ultimate goals they had been fighting for have not been sacrificed for the peace agreement. But at the same time, the political leadership has to assist the opponents and bring them to the negotiating table. By delivering their own people, if the leaders do not get it right, they run the risk of losing their own followers. But if they do not assist their opponents, they risk the collapse of the transition to peace and stability. In effect, for a smoother transition and a way out from a protracted conflict, the political leadership needs to build Sun Tzu's golden bridge.

As mentioned before, leadership may be part of the problem itself. Hence, change of leadership may be a necessary element for a successful transition out of a crisis and/or a conflict. But, then, change of leadership may also be facilitated by the transition process, which is why leadership and its role is also situational. Most leaders like to lead, and if any change risks altering the status quo, they will not be keen to help. As such, they can prioritize leadership survivability over transition and conflict resolution. Plato feared that even leaders who intended to lead in a moral way would be corrupted by the system and, since leaders were essential to the health of the community, a corrupted leader would inevitably destroy his own community and organization.[22] As such, more often than not, pragmatically there has to be a coincidence of personal wants and a leader's duty in order for leaders to remain altruistic and try their best for the higher good. That is why what a leader wants as a person has to coincide with what the followers want and what the country in transition needs.

Burns makes a clear distinction between leadership and the exercise of naked power. However, influence, although it is not a true imperative force, can play an important part in the practice of leadership.

Influence elicits voluntary compliance and agreement. As mentioned in the Introduction, leadership involves decision. Either alone or in partnership with others, leaders select among alternative perspectives available. Afterwards leaders use their personal resources and those of the organization to engage and motivate others to implement their decisions. Kotter's eight-step change process highlights the importance of a narrative and of communication in the change process. Through effective communication, potential misunderstandings and fear of disadvantages can be avoided, and the urgency of the change can only be emphasized by strong communication between leaders and followers. As mentioned earlier, narratives do not arise spontaneously, but they are strategic because "they are deliberately constructed or reinforced out of the ideas and thoughts that are already current."[23] Narratives are compelling story lines which can explain events convincingly and from which inferences can be drawn. However, as the focus of the research is on transitional process, certain questions arise: How can old narratives be reconciled with new realities? What happens when old narratives cannot explain complex new realities in transitional processes?

Necessity for Leadership Survivability.

Change does not come easy for leaders. Power is not something tangible, but it is a relationship which is constantly changing. These changes can be beyond the control of the leaders, which in turn is why change does not come easy for leaders. As mentioned earlier, asymmetric leadership in transitional processes are by definition transformational. However, the key issue is to what extent asymmetric leadership can maintain its transformative stance, in view of the fact that this would be in contrast to the very survival of that leadership. More precisely, as soon as the transitional process is initiated and the new regime and structures are formed, further change is needed as the leader now would have to move "from guiding the political system in introducing new structures, to working within those structures."[24]

In reality, however, more often than not, asymmetric leadership turns from revolutionary and pro-change to conservative, in the sense of preserving the status quo. The continued presence of a leader during a transition process may undermine the ability of the emerging regime to be formed by restricting opportunities for the normalization of politics. In other words, leaders have to be prepared to move from the foreground to the background, which asymmetric leadership might find even more challenging, given the unequal dynamic in the relationship between asymmetric leadership and traditional leadership. Thus, the success of asymmetric leadership depends on the ability to adapt constantly and to maneuver between competing forces and lead through change, while bargaining and compromising where necessary to maintain stability. As G. Breslauer highlights, "rare is the leader who is able to succeed in both, system destruction and system building."[25] To this end, "a breakthrough may be required to undo old structures . . . but numerous and repeated follow-up initiatives are required to put new structures in place and to build legitimacy for the new order."[26]

In protracted conflicts, leaders change because they either "see the light" of new realities or they "feel the heat" in the sense that they feel the pressure either from their own side as well as from the opposing side. If, for political leaders, gambling for survival is more important than what the state wants and needs, their decisionmaking will be affected accordingly. As mentioned previously, there has to be a combination of personal and professional goals for a leader to remain selfless and self-sacrificing, but empirically it is known that leaders base decisionmaking not just on the probability of being removed, but also the manner and consequences of becoming redundant. In point of fact, as the ability of leaders to call on their followers to support the reform program decreases, the more the leaders shift from transformation to a more transactional leadership type. As argued already, a leader may shift from transactional to transformational leadership style, depending on the situation. The reasons for changes from one style of leadership to another may vary, but it may also result from the loss of faith from followers in the ability of the leader to lead effectively in the case of the transformative leader.[27]

For a leader, for instance, the decision to continue or terminate a conflict will depend in part on the anticipated consequences for the leader's personal fate. In the early-1930s, the king of Siam, Prajadhipok, took out unemployment insurance with French and British insurance companies. Having failed to suppress the newly formed constitutional government, he accepted his ouster and collected on the policies. In his Book Eight, Thucydides describes how the overriding concern for personal safety influenced the oligarchy on whether to continue the war. The first aim was to preserve the oligarchy and maintain control over the allies, the second aim was to hold on to the fleet and fortifications of Athens and retain independence, and the third aim was not to be in a position of being the first to be destroyed by a reconstituted democracy. In the end, the oligarchy preferred to call in the enemy, give up the fleet and the fortifications, and make any deal for the future of Athens, provided they had their lives guaranteed. Political leaders who are afraid of losing power through forcible means have less to lose from initiating or prolonging a conflict. After all, leaders who are fighting for their own survival do not need to win, but to just avoid defeat. As Samuel Huntington advocates, "do not prosecute, do not punish, do not forgive, and, above all, do not forget."[28] Leaders may have vested interests in the status quo, and policies may be chosen with an eye to their continued stay in office. In an effort to avoid personal punishment, the leader will try to prolong staying in office, in which case the leader's effort will be to maintain the status quo, even if the present and future are left in limbo, in order to avoid punishment.

In 2007, the businessman Mo Ibrahim established the homonymous prize for Achievement in African leadership. The prize consists of $5 million initial payment over 10 years and thereafter a $200,000 annual payment for life to African leaders who improve the economy, security, and education, and successfully transfer power to their successors. The prize is supposed to be awarded each year to a democratically elected leader who governed well, raised living standards, and then voluntarily left office; but there has not been a winner for about 2 years. The idea is to promote development by changing the incentives that drive political leaders in and out of office. Development and prosperity direct leaders to good governance which, in turn, directs how leaders strike a balance between private gains and public benefits to pursue political careers. Perpetually sponsoring aid and development projects do not alter positively how leaders rule. Foreign support reduces a leader's incentive to negotiate an inclusive distribution of power. At times, there is suppression of entry to power by control from the top, with advancement based on loyalty to the top leader. For a successful transition and effective governance, the focus must be on how to institutionalize domestic accountability rather than external accountability to donors. After all, effective governance can gradually and in a cooperative manner be built, it cannot be imposed.

Instability and crises may provide leaders with unique opportunities to deal with the actors most threatening to the leader's survival. For instance, in Mao Zedong's China, there were five armies loyal to the five heads. Mao Zedong drafted from each of these armies to send to the Korean War. These units were rotated back to China on regular intervals, but were not returned to their original army. At the end of the Korean War, the five armies were merged into one. In this way, Mao removed the four generals from their positions of personal power that could pose a threat to his leadership.

A further challenge of asymmetric leadership is how a leadership can foster an emergent structure in an organization that would help achieve the ultimate goals of the organization, but without the leader creating passive followers following some vision or without creating followers that could challenge their very leadership in the future. To an extent, leadership survivability is vital for internal and external purposes. If there is frequent leadership change, there is no continuity, and it is very difficult to build relationships that would facilitate a smooth transition to peace and stability. Internally, within the organization, lack of leadership continuity can cause uncertainty and lack of commitment and abandonment of what is seen as the fight for the cause. Given that one of the roles of leadership is to build relationships externally, the frequent change of leadership also causes uncertainty and lack of commitment to a peaceful transition process. Internally, a leader has a unitary role and should help to avoid, among other things, dissension and spoiler groups.

However, there appears to be a couple of paradoxes. To fulfill a unitary role, a leader would need to show moderation and openness. But during a protracted conflict and the initial phase of transformation, moderate leaders, with possibly a more pragmatic outlook, fail and fall victims to their own side. The second paradox is that the stronger the leadership, the more likely the survival of a transitional process; but the stronger the leadership, the less the need for compromise and concession in order to achieve this process. Therefore, it becomes a risk for leaders to try and regulate a conflict or a crisis, as it can weaken their position within and between conflicting parties. As such, the early stages of transition are a balancing act. Furthermore, often most relationship building opportunities and peer-learning becomes more limited immediately after the signing of an agreement, because each side tries to find its own space under the new circumstances. Leadership has to be flexible enough to push its constituents in the interests of transition and peace but not push too far to lose support and commitment from the followers.

ENDNOTES - CHAPTER 3

1. K. S. Cameron and R. E. Quinn, *Diagnosing and Changing Organizational Culture: Based on the Competing Values Framework*, Hoboken, NJ: John Wiley & Sons, 2011.

2. J. Blondel, *Political Leadership: Towards a General Analysis*, London, UK: Sage Publications, 1987, pp. 7-8.

3. Russ Marion and Mary Uhl-Bien "Leadership in Complex Organizations," *The Leadership Quarterly*, Vol. 12, 2001, p. 407.

4. Bernd Horn and Allister MacIntyre, eds., *In Pursuit of Excellence: International Perspectives of Military Leadership*, Winnipeg, Canada: Canadian Defence Academy Press, 2006, p. 103.

5. Stephen Rosen, "Thinking about Military Innovation," *Winning the Next War: Innovation and the Next Military*, Ithaca, NY: Cornell University Press, 1995, p. 8.

6. G. Yukl, *Leadership in Organizations*, Westford, MA: Pearson Education Ltd, 2013.

7. G. Greenwald, Chap. 9, *Leadership and Followership*, London, UK: Sage Publications, 2007, p. 232.

8. M. P. Follett, "The Giving of Orders," J. M. Shafritz and J. S. Ott, eds., *Classics of Organization Theory*, Belmont, CA: Wadsworth Publishing Company, 1996, pp. 156-162.

9. Jean Lipman-Blumen, *The Allure of Toxic Leaders: Why We Follow Destructive Bosses and Corrupt Politicians – And How We Can Survive Them*, Oxford, UK: Oxford University Press, 2005, p. 14.

10. É. Durkheim, *De la division du travail social (The Division of Labour in Society)*, French Ed., Charleston, SC: Nabu Press, 2011.

11. Max Weber, *Economy and Society*, Vol. 1, Berkeley, CA: University of California Press, 1978.

12. *Ibid*.

13. See Max Weber, "Types of Authority," Barbara Kellerman, ed., *Political Leadership: A Source Book*, Pittsburgh, PA: University of Pittsburgh Press, 1986, pp. 232-244.

14. James MacGregor Burns, *Leadership*, New York: Harper and Row, 1978.

15. *Ibid*.

16. Terry L Price, "The Ethics of Authentic Transformational Leadership," *Leadership Quarterly*, Vol. 14, No. 1, 2003, pp. 67-81.

17. Niccolo Machiavelli, *The Prince* (Penguin Classics), New York: Penguin Books, 1961.

18. Oren Harari, *The Leadership Secrets of Colin Powell*, New York: McGraw-Hill, 2002, pp. 168, 178.

19. Karl Popper, *The Logic of Scientific Discovery*, London, UK: Routledge, 1959.

20. K. Grint, *Leadership: Limits and Possibilities*, London, UK: Palgrave/Macmillan, 2005.

21. S. Kierkegaard, *Papers and Journals: Selection*, London, UK: Penguin Books, 1996.

22. Plato, *Republic*.

23. L. Freedman, *Transformation of Strategic Affairs*, London, UK: International Institute of Strategic Studies, 2006.

24. Thomas O'Brien, *The Role of the Transitional Leader: A Comparative Analysis of Adolfo Suarez*, Melbourne, Australia: University of Melbourne, 2007; and Boris Yeltsin, *Leadership*, Vol. 3, No. 4, pp. 419-432, especially p. 423.

25. G. Breslauer, *Gorbachev and Yeltsin as Leaders*, New York: Cambridge University Press, 2002, p. 263.

26. *Ibid.*, p. 270.

27. O'Brien, pp. 419-432, especially p. 420.

28. Samuel Huntington, *Third Wave: Democratization in the Late Twentieth Century*, Norman, OK: University of Oklahoma Press, 1993, p. 231.

CHAPTER 4

ASYMMETRIC LEADERSHIP AND TRANSITIONAL PROCESSES

Anastasia Filippidou

This chapter examines whether the role of asymmetric leadership in transitional processes is to protect and safeguard the interests of their own followers or whether asymmetric political leadership transcended self-interest and aims to make peace at all costs. The chapter argues that asymmetric leadership plays multiple roles which often appear incompatible and contradictory.

As examined in Chapter 2, transformational, transactional, and charismatic leadership have been used to explain the leadership of successful social reforms and leadership of transitions from colonial rule and dependence to independence.[1] It is known empirically that political leaders can act as triggers to escalate violence during conflicts but also during peace processes.[2] Similarly, empirically it is also known that political transitions and peace processes might be instigated and supported by the people, but they were made and established by political elites. In point of fact, generally those who lead have mattered more than they possibly should. Although asymmetric leadership in transitional processes is by definition transformative, as it involves moving from one regime to another through the reforming of social and structural relations,[3] this book has emphasized that it is difficult to determine that any single type of leadership is better than another in every situation. Thus, it is apparent that some leadership styles are likely to be more effective in certain situations, and that the really effective leader is one who is able to determine the context of the situation and use the most effective leadership behavior required at the time. After all, leaders in transitional processes have to be at the same time creators and destructors, what J. Schumpeter referred to, albeit in relation to capitalist development, as "incessantly destroying the old one, incessantly creating a new one."[4] Therefore, political leadership of radical political movements during transition processes is often contradictory in style and substance, owing to its asymmetric nature and the circumstances surrounding it. This pragmatically contradictory style depends on the situation, and the issue may make leaders both dogmatic and concessionary, traditionalist and modernizers, idealists and pragmatists, transactional and transformational. This type of leadership is irregular and varying, and it has to be able to adjust and adapt constantly in order to compensate for the unequal dynamic of asymmetric leadership.

Transitional processes have no simple solutions because they are complex. That is, their solution depends on the wider context and, as such, on a variety of interdependent issues and elements. The solution of one issue can have an effect on another issue, or it can generate a new problem. As a result, this interdependence of issues makes a transitional process unique, while uniqueness and complexity can render a transitional process unsolvable. The complexity of the process makes collective agreement more important than getting the right answer. Complex problems, as K. Grint argues, require political collaboration and the role of the leadership is to ask the right questions.[5] Adding to the complexity is the fact that, during a transition process, there is a decrease in the strength of formal institutional structures, as these would be undergoing changes in order to meet the new situation. Moreover, a political vacuum during the transition phase would increase the possibility of conflict, with the participating parties in the transition process viewing the uncertain future outcome as an opportunity to establish a better position for themselves.

For a transitional process to stand a chance to be successful, there has to be a broadly accepted need for change. Understandably, the broader this acceptance the better the chances for success become. The acknowledgment of the need for change also requires a viable way out from the crisis, as well as valid spokespersons.[6] In light of the fact that participation and membership in radical political movements is predominantly voluntary, there also has to be a realistic time scale to achieve these changes. If not, the membership's commitment to the cause of the movement may start faltering. A transitional process will need an end, even if this is symbolic and, as leadership is a relationship between leaders and followers, a transitional process is the responsibility of both leaders and followers.

Leadership often has a negative connotation in transitional processes. Violent conflict is often the result of ruthless leaders who, out of greed for power and resources, exploit their people. Furthermore, despite the different types of leadership discussed in this book, the concept of leadership as such is an hierarchical and authoritarian one relying upon coercion, while leaders can have personal vested interests in the status quo. However, if the situation is untenable, leaders may choose to change or change their aims in order to maintain the status quo.

CHANGE CHALLENGES

It is noteworthy that the outcome of a transitional process is not guaranteed, and it is possible for this process to stall, go backwards, or consolidate in a nondemocratic form.[7] Leading and managing organizations in dynamic and changing situations require leaders that embrace change. In an increasingly interdependent world, even in peaceful environments, leaders and followers are confronted constantly with the challenge of change. Understandably, in transitional situations this challenge is felt even more intensely. The transitional phase is, by nature, a time of intense fluidity as the rules and structures of the preceding regime are eradicated and new ones are developed and implemented in their stead. This transition denotes that there is a reduction in the strength of formal institutional structures, as these are changed and reformed to meet the new situation. Structures and institutions of the previous regime are abolished and replaced by new institutions, and also can provide an opportunity for leaders, but it can simultaneously jeopardize leaders. However, the longer this limbo and vacuum remains, the higher the risk for conflict, with participants seeing the uncertain future as an opportunity to establish a better position for themselves.

J. Kotter's eight-step change process includes establishment of a sense of urgency; creation of a guiding coalition (persuade followers and lead change); development of a strategy and vision (foundation for change); communication of the vision (inclusive interaction); empowering followers (removal of possible obstacles); creation of short-term benefits (motivation and sense of victory); consolidation and development of change (long-term change); and anchoring changes in the culture (values and vision).[8]

As mentioned already, a major challenge for transitional leaders is the role they have in demolishing and building at the same time in a constantly changing environment internally and externally. After a transition, structures and institutions are removed and are replaced by new equivalents. The effectiveness of leaders is based on the ability to introduce successfully and establish these new rules and structures, while ensuring their stability and longevity. These changes can jeopardize the very role of the leader, hence quite understandably, transitional leaders may try to safeguard their own political survival. As such, political leadership in transitional processes is not always a wholly positive phenomenon. Moreover, often divided communities chose to give their support to more radical and polarizing leaders, whose motivations are not always altruistic either in conflict or in subsequent peace processes. Communities do this because these kind of leaders, with their strong ideas, can make followers feel more secure in an already uncertain and volatile environment.

Regarding leadership survivability and transitions to peace processes, Bernard Bass subdivides transformationalism into two distinct types: true transformational and pseudo-transformational leadership.[9] Truly transformational leaders, according to Bass, either align public interest with their own interests or else sacrifice their own interests for the common good. These leaders envisage an attainable future for their followers and their community, which is why narrative and vision are important elements for asymmetric leadership in transitional processes. On the contrary, pseudo-transformational leaders adopt the rhetoric of public interest, but in reality their own self-interest takes precedence.

As discussed earlier, one of the main elements of asymmetric leadership is its adaptability to the circumstances. To paraphrase Gabriel Sheffer, this adaptability is the result of:

> a fresh scrutinizing of the real world; dissatisfaction with the reality that is observed; clear notions about desired changes in existing systems, goals and strategies for change; and dedication to implementing these changes.[10]

All this makes asymmetric leadership a very proactive form of leadership, but at the same time it puts leadership in a position of constantly trying to strike a balance from one element and issue to another.

The need to influence might necessitate political leaders to act in different and at times in contradictory ways at different phases of a peace process. Leading change remains one of the most important, and at the same time most difficult, leadership responsibilities. G. Yukl argues that efforts to implement change are more likely to be successful if a leader "understands the reasons for resistance to change, sequential phases in the change process, different types of change, and the importance of using appropriate models for understanding organizational problems."[11] As Barry Posen argues, it takes time and effort for organizations to unlearn and then relearn.[12] This is supported by the fact that it is the need to keep the organization aligned with changes within the environment that redefines the purpose for which the people, its internal constituents, must facilitate the revised way of doing things.

Change is often associated with uncertainty, and uncertainty is very pervasive within the strategic environment relative to time, place, and space. Radical political organizations prefer to reduce uncertainty in order to maintain commitment from the followers, and it is for this reason they codify solutions as constitutions and manifestos. Still, radical political organizations often find it difficult to conceptualize and implement changes within the organization, and they become content with structures and principles that served them in the past. From the followers' and members' perspective, conformity to current practices and the accepted norms are requirements for upward mobility, and those who are part of the system become fully aware that the logics of consequentialism and appropriateness requires their unwavering loyalty to the organization and to their leaders.[13] Consequently, leaders have to think broadly in terms of systems, nonlinear effects, and network forces, and hence feed the natural, bottom-up dynamics of emergence, innovation, and fitness.[14]

RIPENESS AND THE ROLE OF LEADERSHIP

The Chinese symbol for crisis is a combination of danger and opportunity. As mentioned already, crises are natural occurrences, and for their effective solution, there is a need to make the best of it. Political leadership is directly related to problem-solving. After all, political leadership means the diagnosis of a problem, the prescription of solutions, and the mobilization of support for needed action.[15] Understandably, the problem-solving quality of leadership is very important in the context of violent conflicts and transitions to peace processes.

Given the uncertainties involved in any transitional process, political leaders at times perceive a process as positive, and another as negative or more risky. This would explain any apparent inconsistencies in their attitudes and behaviors toward a peace process which they might be a part. During transitional processes, there is often a contradiction between the expectation placed on leaders to do the right thing in often a self-sacrificing manner and to secure the best outcome possible for their own organization on the one hand, and what is actually best for the country in general, on the other. Often the personal needs and interests of a leader or the interests of the specific organization are in direct contrast with the interests of the wider community. What is more, often in transitional processes, the leaders with the most influence are the more radical ones, which renders a transitional process even more challenging. Furthermore, during a transitional process leaders have to be prepared to become more inclusive, and instead of focusing on a very limited group of leaders, they have to broaden the number of political players who could help shape a peace process and drive it forward. Finally, during transitional processes, there is often a clear contradiction between the need to build relationships between the different political leaders within the context, however, of the adversarial nature of peace processes. In other words, transitional leaders have to build workable relationships with their adversaries, while at the same time, they need to fight for their interests and that of their organization.

According to I.W. Zartman, a conflict must reach a ripe point in order for efforts to resolve that conflict to be fruitful and to lead to a successful transition to peace.[16] Now for a conflict to reach ripeness, Zartman argues that the conflicting parties have to commonly accept that there is a mutually hurting stalemate, a viable way out, and a valid and commonly accepted spokesperson. For a mutually hurting stalemate

(MHS) the leadership of the conflicting parties will have to realize and be prepared to accept that they cannot defeat the other side, but also at the same time, they do not want to admit defeat. However, an MHS is only an element of a transition process. There also has to be the option of a viable way out. If not, the recognition of an MHS can create a vacuum which then may be filled by elements that can escalate the conflict. Like the MHS, this viable way out also has to be commonly accepted by the conflicting parties. The valid spokesperson is either a leader or somebody who will be playing a leading role. In this context, the leadership is cultivating relationships between key players.

In an increasingly interdependent world, transition can be achieved and stability can be built through networks and, as mentioned before, leadership signifies a relationship and a relationship flourishes based on co-existence. A political strength of a stable government is in the leaders who have stakes in the government and in the network of supporters. Distributing power and giving local and grassroot leaders a stake in the regime, strengthens the regime, and reduces the need for foreign support.

NEGATIVE AGREEMENT VS. POSITIVE DISAGREEMENT

Since no leader has the knowledge and power to lead effectively on his own, leadership is a collective affair. Thus, for effective and successful leadership, it is imperative to achieve agreement and constructive dissent, if necessary, instead of disagreement and destructive consent. Destructive consent as Grint argues is "the bedfellow of irresponsible followership" and an inadequate frame for addressing protracted and complex problems.[17] Groupthink, which is the tendency for groups and communities to suppress internal dissent, is dominant among groups under duress and pressure. Furthermore, nondominant individuals and groups find it difficult, if not impossible, to break out of the groupthink and to express their dissent—constructive or not—and to break into leadership positions within established organizations and groups. On the other hand, constructive dissenters are willing to stand up to their leaders and express their disagreement to a wrong decision. The argument for constructive dissent is not for followers to disagree constantly with their leaders but to dissent if the leaders are deemed to be acting against the interests of the organization and the community as such.

As stated in the introduction thesis of the research, there is a need for a constant balancing of different characteristics of leadership and for an adjustment of leadership styles to continuously changing situations. When followers, for instance, lose their motivation and do not want to support the transitional process, political leaders have to alter their leadership style to a transactional one instead of transformational leadership. This supports the thesis of the research that leaders need a variety of leadership styles and models. D. Goleman poignantly argues that leaders "must play their leadership style like a pro—using the right one at just the right time and in the right measure."[18] This is what Ronald Heifetz categorizes as adaptive leadership.[19]

ENDNOTES - CHAPTER 4

1. See, for instance, Betty Glad, "Passing the Baton: Transformational Political Leadership from Gorbachev to Yeltshin; from de Klerk to Mandela," *Political Psychology*, Vol. 17, No. 1, 1996, pp. 1-28; and Colin Barker, Alan Johnson, and Michael Lavalette, eds., *Leadership and Social Movements*, Manchester, United Kingdom (UK): Manchester University Press, 2001.

2. M. E. Brown, "Ethnic and Internal Conflicts: Causes and Implications," Chester Crocker, Fen Osler Hampson, and Pamela Aall, eds., *Turbulent Peace: The Challenges of Managing International Conflict*, Washington, DC: United States Institute of Peace, p. 220.

3. Thomas O'Brien, "The Role of the Transitional Leader: A Comparative Analysis of Adolfo Suarez and Boris Yeltsin," *Leadership*, Vol. 3, No. 4, pp. 419-432, especially p. 422.

4. J. Schumpeter, *Capitalism, Socialism and Democracy*, London, UK: Routledge, 1976, p. 83.

5. K. Grint, interview, available from *www.som.cranfield.ac.uk/ som/dinamic-content/media/knowledgeinterchange/booksummaries/ Arts%20of%20Leadership%20-%20Part%202/Transcript.pdf*.

6. See I. W. Zartman, *Peacemaking in International Conflict: Methods and Techniques*, Washington, DC: United States Institute of Peace, 2007; and J. Galtung, *Peace by Peaceful Means: Peace and Conflict, Development and Civilization*, Oslo, Norway: Peace Research Institute Oslo, 1996.

7. M. McFaul, "The Fourth Wave of Democracy and Dictatorship: Non-Competitive Transitions in the Post-Communist World," *World Politics*, 2002, Vol. 54, No. 2, pp. 212-244.

8. J. Kotter, *Leading Change*, Boston, MA: Harvard Business School Press, 1996.

9. Bernard Bass and P. Steidlmeier, "Ethics, Character and Authentic Transformational Leadership Behavior," *Leadership Quarterly*, Vol. 10, No. 2, 1999, pp. 181-217.

10. Gabriel Sheffer, "Moshe Sharett: The Legacy of an Innovative Moderate Leader," Gabriel Sheffer, ed., *Innovative Leaders in International Politics*, Albany, NY: State University of New York Press, 1993, p. 85.

11. G. Yukl, *Leadership in Organizations*, Upper Saddle River, NJ: Prentice Hall, 2006, p. 285.

12. Barry Posen, *Sources of Military Doctrine: France, Britain and Germany between the World Wars*, Ithaca, NY: Cornell University Press, 1984, pp. 34-80.

13. Terry Terriff, "Innovate or Die: Organizational Culture and the Origins of Maneuver Warfare in the United States Marine Corps," *Journal of Strategic Studies*, Vol. 29, No. 3, June 2006, pp. 478-479.

14. Russ Marion and Mary Uhl-Bien, "Leadership in Complex Organizations," *The Leadership Quarterly*, Vol. 12, 2001, p. 403.

15. R. C. Tucker, *Politics as Leadership*, Columbia, MO: University of Missouri Press, 1981.

16. Zartman.

17. K. Grint, *Leadership: Limits and Possibilities*, London, UK: Palgrave/Macmillan, 2005.

18. D. Goleman, "Leadership that Gets Results," *Harvard Business Review*, March-April 2000, pp. 78-90, especially p. 90.

19. R. Heifetz, ed., *Practice of Adaptive Leadership: Tools and Tactics for Changing Your Organisation and the World*, Boston, MA: Cambridge Leadership Associates, 2009.

PART II:

LEADERSHIP IN VOLATILE AND TRANSITIONAL SITUATIONS CASE STUDIES

CHAPTER 5

THE CASE OF LEBANON

Elias Hanna

INTRODUCTION

Leadership in Lebanon is directly related to the volatile nature of its political structure. Throughout history, the degrees of volatility have determined the kind of leaders the Lebanese society has produced. During times of turmoil, leaders have found legitimacy in their religious, sectarian, or even feudal backgrounds. Also, the political influence of various foreign powers has produced a certain class of leaders. Furthermore, the leaders that the recurrent civil wars have produced are by militias that derived their legitimacy through arms.

While teaching students the history of Lebanon and the Middle East from the Ottoman Empire era until modern times, including the independence period and the creation of Greater Lebanon, the common and recurrent questions from my students are: When will Lebanon be a normal country? When will we have the luxury of planning for the future? When will the brain drain stop? When will we stop being a buffer state and a battle ground for the region? When will we be able to break the cycle of civil wars? My answer is that this is the normal status of Lebanon. Unfortunately, the idea about Lebanon being the Switzerland of the Middle East is a myth. Could it be the tyranny of geography? Does the geographic location of Lebanon make it volatile or unstable? Or is it the constituencies that form Lebanon, or the political culture? Is it the lack of experience with the imposed political entity? Is Lebanon a nation-state? Is it the regional environment? History has taught us that political upheavals in Lebanon follow a certain framework and a pattern cycle. If we need to understand the history of Lebanon that oscillates between anarchy, chaos, and quasi-stability, it is a must to comprehend in depth the framework as well as the pattern mentioned earlier.

I would like to discuss two theories that explain and help analyze the aforementioned patterns. The first is called the theory of the circle and the arrow, which means: history repeats itself in Lebanon, a politically volatile country, where civil wars are a part of the Lebanese life and culture. The variables are the context: political, economic, and social. Thus the recurrent civil wars that arise from different dynamics, according to the variables and the context, show that the elites and leadership are the consequence of the quasi-stability and the volatility. (See Figure 5-1.)

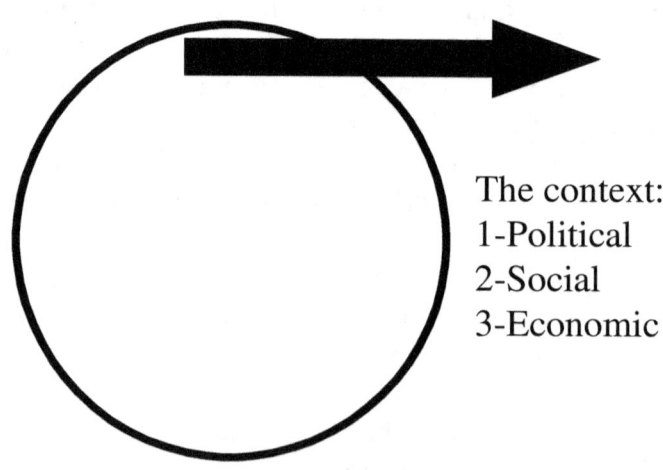

The context:
1-Political
2-Social
3-Economic

Figure 5-1. Context.

In this chapter, we will discuss the geopolitics of Lebanon and determine its geopolitical imperatives. The application of the theory or the framework of the previously mentioned cycle on key periods of the history of Lebanon such as civil wars, invasions, occupations, and quasi-stable times is also discussed. Accordingly, we will shed light on the role and creation of leadership during these periods, and discuss how they acquired their legitimacy and how they behaved during a quasi-permanent state of crisis.

THE GEOPOLITICS OF LEBANON

Geopolitics is a study of the influence of such factors as geography, economics, and demography, on the politics and especially the foreign policy of a state.[1] The geopolitics of Lebanon depends totally on its location. Lebanon is the linchpin between east and west,[2] rather it is the main passage between those two worlds, even though we are witnessing the third historical revolution, the technological one,[3] where geography is starting to become irrelevant.

A look from above God's eye, as we say in geopolitics, locates Lebanon on the main historical axis of instability, volatility, and chaos. The Fertile Crescent (see Map 5-1[4]) is the starting and vital point, the bridgehead to enter this crescent, for an empire coming from the west, as well as the ultimate goal for any empire that is moving from the east and willing to project power toward the west.

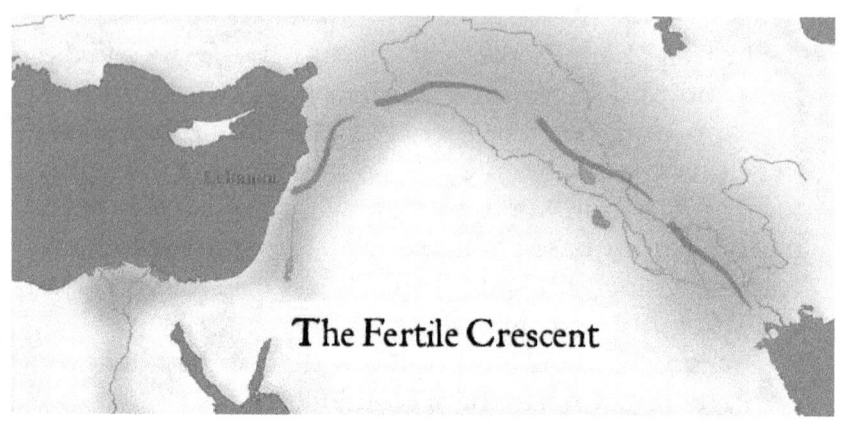

Map 5-1. The Fertile Crescent.

This Fertile Crescent was historically and still is a buffer area among the major regional empires. It used to be, and still is, the battleground where accounts are settled—compare it to present times. In the modern era, we may add Israel as a major regional player (see Map 5-2).

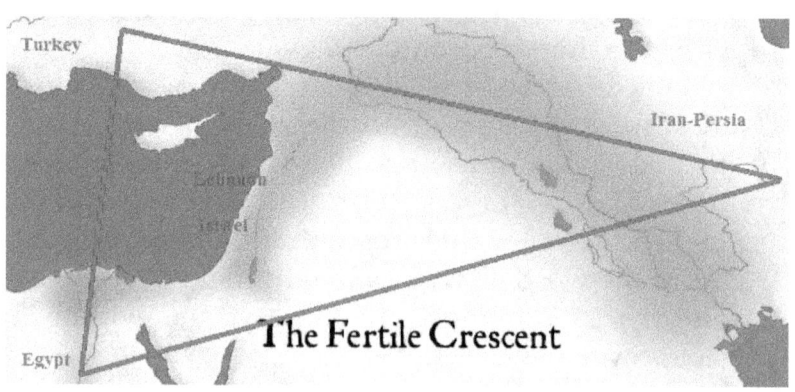

Map 5-2. Buffer Zone.

In this realm, it is necessary to discuss the second theory, the Theory of the Three Ring Model, followed by the pattern of the history of Lebanon as a major consequence of this theory.

The Three Ring Model.[5]

This theory or framework is a guideline and a road map that leads us into the analysis of the history of Lebanon. It is a way to explain Lebanon's phenomena. The past history of Lebanon is best understood by using the so-called theory of the Three Ring Model. The Three Ring Model, see Figure 5-2, if well used and fed by historical factors, may lead to discern a certain pattern of civil wars in Lebanon, how they occur, how they are resolved, and, last but not least, how the political solution is usually imposed on Lebanon. It also depicts how, by default, leadership is created.

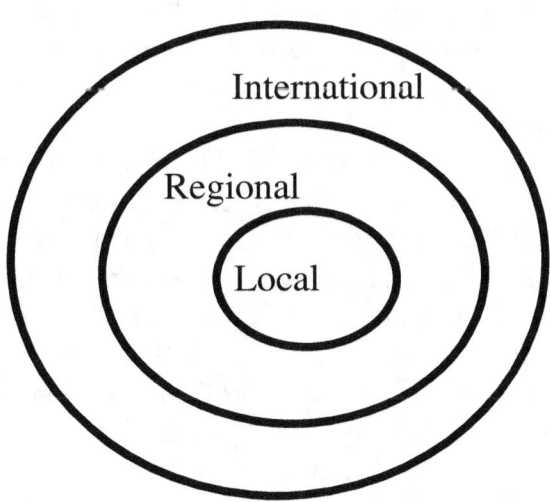

Figure 5-2. Three Ring Model.

The first ring is the outer ring and is used to determine the international players that affect the situation in Lebanon, how the world order is set and interacts, how it relates to internal dynamics, and how it influences Lebanon.

The second ring is the regional one where the regional players interact within the realm of a multipolar, bipolar, or, as at the time of this writing, perhaps nonpolar world order.[6] This ring will display the regional order, alliances, and enmity; the stakes; the rules of the game; and last, but not least, where Lebanon fits, which leads us to the last inner ring of the theory.

The third ring is the local Lebanese inner ring where the effects of the dynamics of conflict or cooperation at the world order level and the regional one are really felt. Thus as a consequence, we can understand what is happening in the world or the region by following and monitoring the micro-political level in Lebanon, and vice versa. In this ring, the civil wars by proxy are waged. By looking deep into this ring, we can discern and analyze the rise of leadership and elites in Lebanon.

Thus, what goes within the international system is directly reflected in the Middle Eastern regional system, and then felt on the Lebanese theater. It has been like this historically, and it will go on until the Lebanese political elites can create a magic solution to shield Lebanon from external influences. Unfortunately, this does not appear likely in the near future. The clearest example in how these circles interact and how they affect the inner circle is the project of the "New Middle East" promoted by former U.S. President George W. Bush, which led to the July 2006 war.[7]

The Pattern in Lebanon's History.

What happens within the dynamics of the Three Ring Model theory will create the following consequences in Lebanon:
- Internal strife under multiple aspects, including secular nationalism, religious or sectarian.
- Possible return of civil war.
- Last, but not least, since Lebanon's political elites historically could not create their own political solutions, a political solution is always imposed on Lebanon.

Going through the first step of the pattern does not really lead to civil war. Civil war could be skipped to go directly to the imposed political solution. In between, a mini-civil war could occur.[8]

Geo-Codes of the Lebanese Imperatives.

After situating Lebanon in the region and discussing the fate of the land of the Cedars, it is a must now to define some geopolitical imperatives and codes. Colin Flint defines vision and codes as follows:

A **vision** is the understanding of a state's national history, character, or even destiny that is stable and is rooted in popular sentiment. The vision is the foundation that is mobilized to 'make sense' of the code.

A **code** is more dynamic — it changes with changing circumstances — and is the product of state elites. It is the foreign policy calculations that are reassessed daily.[9]

In the case of Lebanon, unfortunately, there is neither vision nor defined and clear geo-codes due to the lack of national unity in defining the vital interests, such as defining the friends and foes of the nation. The threats of which can be inflicted on Lebanon by both enemies and friends/allies alike. We neither have a grand strategy in Lebanon, nor a document issued at the official level dealing with the national security strategy. Regretfully, all we have in the official statement are a few sentences that address national security that were written by newly formed governments to gain the confidence of the legislature.[10]

As mentioned by Flint, the relationships between vision and geo-codes and (as discussed earlier) the Three Ring framework, it is useful and possible to discern now some geo-codes and imperatives for Lebanon, having in mind those geo-codes are not like a silver bullet that will solve all Lebanon's ills. However, we can consider them like a road map since they are dynamics and change according to the context in the circle and arrow theory discussed earlier.

- The unity of the land.
- A political consensus on how to distribute wealth and power.
- Stop being a buffer state for the global and regional dynamics, thus stopping the cycle of civil wars and the pattern of imposing political solutions on the area as well.
- Lebanon is not a capital maker and provider, rather it is a capital manager and consumer of services. We need the foreign direct investments to keep the country rolling on the way of prosperity. In addition, we need to also keep the hard currency coming into Lebanon through

remittances[11] from the Lebanese diaspora in the Arab World as well as in other regions. Thus, we must be, and stay, liberally oriented and have no conflict and enmity with any country in the Arab World. As Michel Chiha has said about Lebanon being a mountain and a sea state, the sea is to keep doing business with the outside world, and the mountain protects the minorities.[12]

SOME PERMANENT FACTS ABOUT THE LEBANESE CASE

Lebanon is considered a fragmented, unstable democracy according to Arend Lijphart.[13] Moreover, the distribution of political power in Lebanon is consociational. It is a consociational democracy based on religious and sectarian dimensions. In addition, stability in such a system necessitates a positive role of the elites. In the Lebanese case, the elites of the subcultures that form the Lebanese fabrics are usually in a competitive mode even within the same culture, religion, or sect.

Lebanon is a main part of the region, especially the Arab World. It is linked to the regional environment, as the brain is a part of the human body. When events occur in Palestine, we feel it all over the Arab world. What makes Lebanon different is the political system, i.e., a democratic country surrounded by authoritarian regimes. Thus, the concept of neutrality for Lebanon is out of the question; hence the relevancy of our Three Ring Model.

The recurrence of the civil wars in Lebanon is due to how the previous war has ended, i.e., the war termination process, or what the scholar Edward Luttwak described as "give war a chance."[14] Negotiated settlements to end the civil war will keep two or more sovereignties among protagonists, and the security dilemma will be enhanced. Thus, the settlement will be temporary and tactical, to survive and prepare to fight another time.

In Lebanon, the slogan to follow after ending a civil war, and the imposition of the political solution, is: "No victor, no vanquished." It is considered as the main platform for reconciliation, though this reconciliation is fake and shallow. Hence, civil wars occurred in 1845, 1860, 1958, and 1975, with numerous mini wars in between.

Last, but not least, the same negative dynamics on Lebanon of the Three Ring Model discussed previously that lead Lebanon to civil war; are the same dynamics that are also positive on Lebanon and will lead Lebanon to terminate the war. Said differently, Lebanon is caught between two dynamics within our theory. One is negative and leads to internal strife and to civil war by consequence. The other is positive and takes Lebanon to the imposed political solution, and to an enforced stability not too far from volatility. Thus, Lebanon is in a lose-lose situation in both dynamics. It is all about the degree of volatility and the amount to be paid in human and material losses.

Civil Wars Seen from the Three Ring Model and Role of Elites.

In 1840-85, Lebanon witnessed a civil war due to the competition in the international system—European powers (United Kingdom [UK], France, Austria), Russia, and the Ottoman Empire. Those powers, if used within our theory of the Three Ring Model, would depict the European Union (EU) powers in the first ring; the Ottoman Empire in the first and second — the regional; and as far as the local ring is concerned — 1st ring — at that time, Mount Lebanon was the political entity, where Druses and Maronites coexisted in a self-ruled status. Due to the competition in the international system, a sectarian civil war broke out in Mount Lebanon.

When the world powers interfered, a political resolution was imposed on Mount Lebanon, Al-Qaimaqamiah.[15] This political system created what we now call the confessional system. The imposed political solution created a new kind of leadership and elites at the inner ring. The qaimaqam governs his district, and there were two districts — Druse and Maronite — aided by a council formed on sectarian basis. The elites of that time could not really protect Mount Lebanon from the recurrent civil war. Civil war reoccurred in 1860.

The 1860 civil war was also sectarian and occurred between the same factions, Druses and Maronites, within the same geographic theater, Mount Lebanon, and spread to Damascus. The same powers interfered, but the Ottoman Empire was the "sick man" at that time, and another political solution was imposed under a new political system, the Al-Moutasarsifiah (see Map 5-3).[16] The elites or the political leaders at the time were chosen by the Ottoman Empire, especially the Al-Moutasarref or the governor, and imposed on Mount Lebanon. The Lebanese Druse and Maronites had no say in choosing their leaders. The Moutasarref had to be a Christian but a non-Maronite proposed by the Ottoman authority, and approved by the greater

European powers. The Governor was aided by a council of 12 members chosen on a sectarian basis.[17] In addition, Mount Lebanon was divided into seven geographic districts.

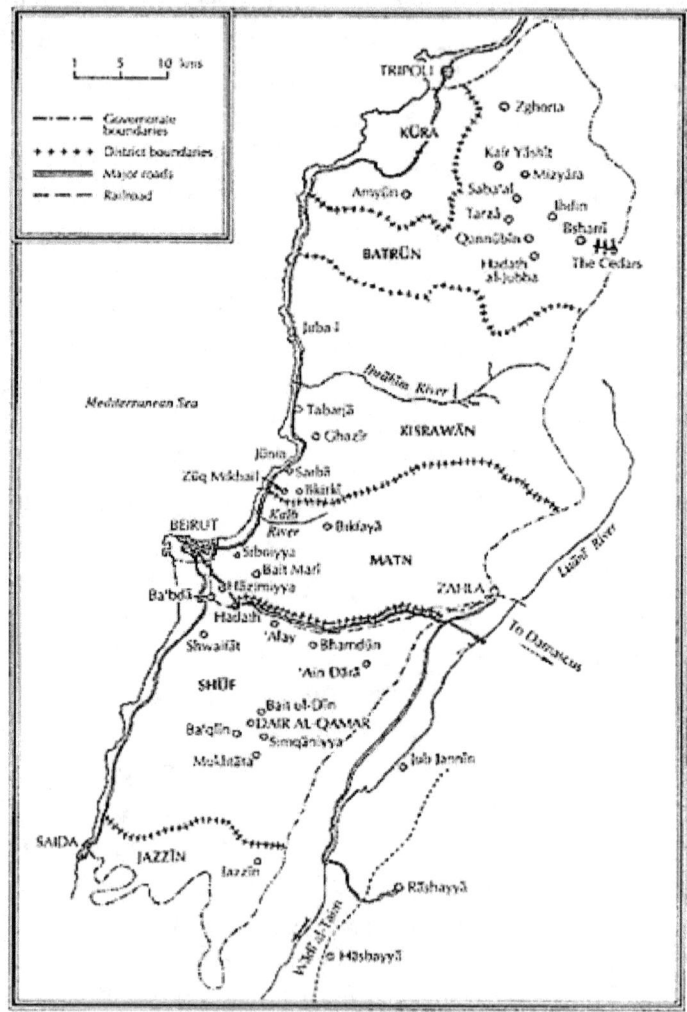

Map 5-3. Map of Al-Moutasarsifiah.

The end of World War I and the collapse of the Ottoman Empire led to the creation of Greater Lebanon in 1920 by the French, represented by General Henri Gouraud. The creation of Greater Lebanon led to an identity crisis for the constituencies of Lebanon. Are we Arabs? Are we Phoenicians? Do we belong to the Arab world, greater Syria? Are we a different civilization? Oriented toward the Western world? Vital identity issues simmered and were the main reasons for fomenting the internal strife within the above mentioned pattern. According to prominent Lebanese historian Albert Hourani, the creation of Greater Lebanon mixed two incompatible ideologies; the ideology of the mountain—of the Christians Maronites—and the ideology of the city—of the coast where the Muslim Sunnis reside.[18] For Hourani, the mountain ideology is insular, superstitious, religious, and populist; hence the distrust of the city, where the ideology is pluralistic which creates internal strife.[19]

Hourani implies several issues. On the one hand, the status of Mount Lebanon under the Ottoman Empire where Christian Maronites coexisted along with the Druse Community for centuries created a certain special *modus vivendi* and *operandi* ideology of the mountain regardless of the two civil wars that had occurred, since we consider them as the by-product of this unique experience between the two sects. Moreover, under Al-Qaimaqamiah and Al-Moutasarsifiah, Mount Lebanon went through a unique political experience of quasi-self-governing, which prepared the people of the mountain, especially the Maronites, to take the helm of Greater Lebanon in 1920 and consider it a nation-state. Last, but not least, Maronites perceive themselves as a separate entity from the region especially from Greater Syria.

On the other hand, the people of the city never went through the same experiences as the people of the mountain. They were mainly governed directly by the Ottoman Empire through the Wali. Moreover, they were mainly Sunni Muslims. Religiously, they looked to the Khalifa in the Astana Ottoman Empire for guidance. They have never experienced any common *modus vivendi* and *operandi* with the Maronites. Last, but not least, they perceive themselves as a part of a wider Arab World and a Muslim world that really goes beyond the border of Lebanon.

When in 1920 Greater Lebanon was created, these two ideologies were put together to the test—imposed political solution—with no previous common experience on how to distribute power and wealth. Also, they were put to the test on how to deal with their geo-strategic environment, whether in war or in peace, since the ideologies are incompatible, hence the permanent internal strife when there is any shift in the regional geopolitical environment (the second ring of the framework). In this period, the main elites that were behind the creation of Greater Lebanon the religious Christian Maronites[20] on the one hand; and on the other, the elites opposing this creation were mainly Sunni under the Arab Nationalism umbrella.

A Turning Point for Lebanon.

After numerous major geopolitical shifts in the regional ring, especially the fall of the Ottoman Empire and the creation of the Arab Nation-State, Lebanon became a de facto country. All parties began to realize that there was no way back, and they had to follow and abide by the new geopolitical game and its consequences of different dynamics in the Three Ring Model.

Therefore, the political elites started to reassess the situation to see how to create a *modus vivendi* among the constituencies of the new nation-state, mainly Christian Maronites and Muslim Sunnis, in order to have a stable and prosperous country. In 1943, an agreement was reached which was called the National Pact.

The main purpose of this pact was really to isolate the inner ring—the local—as much as possible from the regional and outer rings. According to the agreement, the Christians would not ask for help from France, and the Muslims will never ask to be reintegrated in Greater Syria. In addition, the distribution of power will follow the ratio 6:5 in favor of the Christians, based on the 1932 census.[21]

Along with the Constitution, written in 1926, the National Pact of 1943 was morally binding for the political elites from both religions to work and cooperate for the stability and prosperity of Lebanon. This continued until 1948 when the Arab world was struck by a major "Black Swan"[22] event that shook its foundations—the creation of the state of Israel.

The Creation of Israel Analyzed through the Three Ring Model.

The creation of Israel is analyzed through the following rings:

- The international ring:
  - The world order was going through a major geopolitical shift, the decline of Great Britain, and the redistribution of power globally; hence the decision of Great Britain to withdraw from Palestine.

- The new world order became bipolar — the United States vs. the Union of Soviet Socialist Republics (USSR).
- The cold war ensued.

- The regional ring:
  - The withdrawal of Great Britain from the region created a vacuum and hence a time of uncertainty.
  - The major defeat of the Arab countries during the 1948[23] war with Israel led to a de facto power in the region called the al-Nakba, a major blow to the Arab countries. The refugee catastrophe ensued from this war,[24] created a burden on host countries. Many wars followed 1956, 1967, 1973, and 1982, and more recently the July 2006 war. After al-Nakba, Arab countries were never politically stable. *Coup d'état* and counter-coups occurred for many years. The military dominated politics in many Arab countries. Finally, the Gamal Abdel Nasser reign in Egypt in1952, under the Pan Arabism umbrella, added salt on Lebanese wounds.

- The Local Ring:
  - At the national level, the National Pact was put to the test on how to really isolate Lebanon from the regional upheaval. The refugee crisis provoked deep communal divisions, critical internal political debate, even ideological controversies, and deep debate on the identity of Lebanon.

The creation of Israel in 1948 led to new dynamics for the Three Ring Model. There was more activity on the regional dimension than on the international one, and, by consequence, political volatility increased in Lebanon.

The rise of Gamal Nasser after the Suez Canal crisis in 1956 and his project to unite the Arab world starting with Syria in 1958 under the banner of the United Arab Republic (UAR), created an internal tension in Lebanon. President Camille Chamoun invoked the Dwight Eisenhower Doctrine[25] and asked for U.S. help. Five thousand U.S. Marines landed on the shores of Lebanon to end a 3-month rebellion. The interference of U.S. Marines in Lebanon was meant to "hit two birds with one stone." On the regional front, it was meant to send a message to Nasser after a *coup d'état* occurred in Iraq, toppling the pro-American monarchy. On the local front, the landing of the Marines created the needed atmosphere to stop the rebellion and deny any interference from the UAR, where Nasser was the de facto president.[26] The imposed political solution after this period of instability was the election of General of the Lebanese Army Fouad Chehab, after a tacit agreement was reached between the United States and Egypt on the new president.[27] Again, Lebanon oscillated between democracy, liberty, volatility, and stability. Once again, stability was imposed.

With Chehab as president, an agreement was reached between Nasser and Chehab to work on the stability of Lebanon, on the condition that Chehab will follow a pro-Nasser foreign policy.[28] The cordial agreement between the two presidents insulated Lebanon from any Arab interference in its internal affairs, especially from the giant neighbor, Syria, but this was temporary. Moreover, this relationship buffered Lebanon from any negative consequences that might occur from the dynamics of the Three Ring Model. Nasser guaranteed the loyalty of the Muslim nationalists in Lebanon to the state. It was a managed stability — a fake and contextual one. When the rules of the game changed, the equation of stability fell, and Nasser's death in 1970 caused the return of the volatile state once again. Thus, the leadership of Lebanon was selected by the international ring and agreed upon by the regional one.

After Chehab, President Charles Helou was chosen, as usual, outside the legal process or the democratic institutions; the Parliamentary election was just a charade. It is said that the election of Helou came after a simple telephone call between previous President Chehab and President Nasser, with some help from the Egyptian ambassador in Beirut, Abdel Hamid Ghaleb.[29]

The Six-Day War of 1967 was another blow to Arab pride, and to the stability of Lebanon. If the first war of 1948 was tagged as Al-Nakba, this war earned the name of Al-Naksa. After the 1967 war, no major Arab state was able to wage a conventional war against Israel. Consequently, at the Khartoum Arab League Summit, the mission to fight Israel was diverted to a nonstate actor, The Palestinian Liberation Organization (PLO). At the summit, 13 Arab countries issued the three No's: No peace, No negotiation, and No recognition. They pledged for the continuation of the struggle against Israel until the return of Palestine.[30]

Since peace was ruled out as a solution at the Khartoum Summit, war became the only way to recover the lost and occupied lands. However, the questions remained: How? Where, and by whom? Once again, Lebanon suffered the consequences of the Arab defeat, and the dynamics of the regional ring laid its heavy weights on the fragile country as the weakest node in the Arab world. Lebanon is the only Arab country with an ideal location to wage an unconventional war on Israel. Hence the 1969 Cairo agreement[31] imposed on Lebanon during the reign of Helou.

The Cairo agreement provided the PLO a platform to attack Israel from Lebanese territories, creating a state within a state.[32] Between the PLO's attacks on Israel and the Israeli retaliation, Lebanon lost its sovereignty, and went to civil war in 1975, followed by an unprecedented and destructive war during the Israeli invasion of 1982. No Lebanese leadership during this critical period was really able to manage the situation positively. Rather, the chairman of the PLO, Yasser Arafat, was a de facto ruler of most of Lebanon, including Beirut and the South. On the other hand, Syria and Israel were using Lebanon as a battleground and a buffer state. The legitimate sate of Lebanon was limited to a small, mostly Christian area.

The civil war of 1975 lasted the longest and was the major factor to redistribute the political power in Lebanon afterwards. The war can be explained according to our framework of the Three Ring Model:

1. The international ring—world order—was at that time bipolar between the USSR and the United States. At this time, the United States was caught in the Vietnam War with no possibility in sight to withdraw.

2. In the regional ring, the October war erupted in 1973, surprising Israel as well as the United States. Israel was attacked by Egypt and Syria in the Sinai and the Golan heights. It was a semi-victory for the Arabs and a semi-defeat for Israel. But the realities after the war proved that Israel was not really invincible and that the Arabs could wage conventional war against

Israel as well, though the qualitative edge was in Israel's favor. The major consequence of the October war was the oil embargoes by the Gulf Arab oil countries. This embargo hit the Western world hard, especially the United States.

According to Lebanese writer Roger J. Azzam, the civil war of 1975 was planned and initiated by former Secretary of State Henry Kissinger and called the Kissinger's plan.[33] In addition to this, American political activist Lyndon Larouche mentioned the same plan by Kissinger to plunge Lebanon into civil war.[34]

Briefly, the plan is as follows:

- Saudi Arabia's King Faisal was behind the oil embargo. He was assassinated by his half brother's son, Faisal bin Musaid, on March 25, 1975.
- The *casus belli* for the October war were the Palestinians. The PLO resided in Lebanon and had taken control over it. On April 13, 1975, the Ain El Rummaneh[35] bus incident occurred, which sparked the fourth civil war.[36] The PLO was destroyed in Lebanon during the 1982 Israeli invasion
- Lebanon was divided between Israel and Syria; a small area was left for the Christians, approximately the old area of Al-Moutasarsifiah as discussed earlier.
- Secret and tacit rules for the game between Israel and Syria were in place, for example, Israel will have the air dominance over Lebanon, while Syria will never militarily cross the Al-Awali River near the city of Sidon, which is the main entrance between the Mount Lebanon district and Southern Lebanon.[37]

- Thus, instead of fighting each other directly, the war between Israel and Syria was fought by proxy on Lebanese land. During this time, Lebanon was in a lose-lose situation.

The human toll of this war was huge, with more than 100,000 people killed. Lebanon was totally destroyed, and geographically partitioned into many sectarian cantons (see Map 5-4).[38] In this plan, the international ring used the Lebanese civil war to solve its geopolitical conundrum and to create a new regional environment where the Palestinian question is weaker after losing its military teeth through the destruction of the PLO.

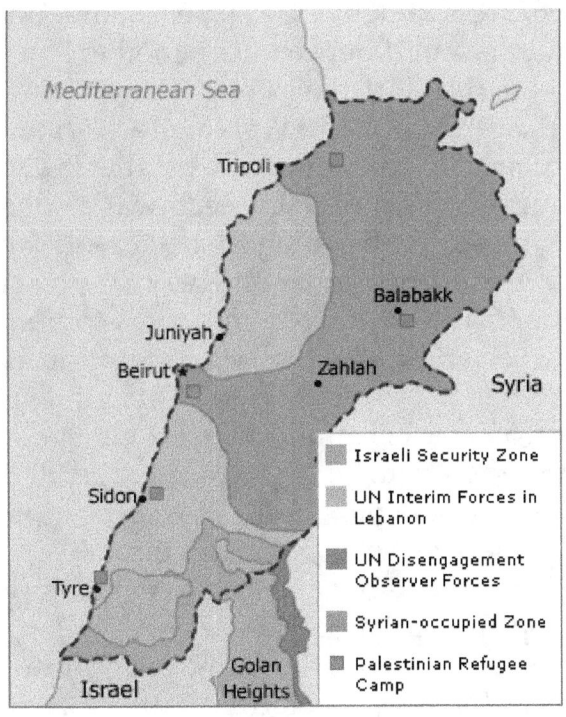

Map 5-4. Division of Lebanon after the Civil War of 1975.

The civil war of 1975 went through many phases; all of which took Lebanon from bad to worse. Moreover, a hidden war went along with the civil war between Arafat and President Hafez Al Assad, on the political control of the Palestinian card. Whoever controlled Palestine would have the upper hand in any peace process, and would be the sole representative of the most crucial Arab issue. Lebanon was used as a battleground for the indirect war between Assad and Arafat, as well as between Assad and the leaders of the whole Arab world, since the PLO was physically and politically in Lebanon, and Syria has the longest borders with Lebanon.

In 1967, Assad delivered a speech announcing the overt military interference in Lebanon to stop the war and protect the Christians from being massacred by the forces of Al Haraka Al Watanieh — National Movement — which was being aided by the PLO.[39] Moreover, the main point in the speech was to deny Israel any part in the partitioning of Lebanon.[40] The entry of Syrian forces into Lebanon had many geopolitical implications and objectives. First was to buffer Syria from the sectarian war that was raging in Lebanon; second was to try to control the PLO and deny Arafat total control over Lebanon; and third, Lebanon would give Syria the strategic depth needed in its struggle with Israel and the possibility of waging a proxy war against Israel without being accountable. In other words, Syria would have plausible deniability.

To stop the bloody civil war in Lebanon, in 1976 the Arabs decided, in the Al Riyadh Arab League conference, to send a deterrent Arab force[41] to end the war, rebuild the Lebanese Army, control the PLO, and restore order between belligerents. This deterrent force, in fact, added salt on Lebanese wounds. Nearly 90 percent of the forces were comprised of the Syrian army. Most of them were already fighting in Lebanon. When war broke out again, the non-Syrian Arab forces left, leaving the bulk of the Arab Deterrent Force (ADF), mostly Syrians, fighting the Lebanese militias, mainly the Christians.

Along with the initiative of the ADF, a new Lebanese President was elected in 1976, Elias Sarkis. As usual, the presidential election in the parliament was prearranged; this phenomenon was to turn into a Lebanese pattern. It is said that the agreement was made between American envoy Dean Brown and Syrian President Assad. Therefore, the situation in Lebanon depended on local and global interference, and their synchronization, whether to stop the civil war or to choose political elites by the same dynamics that had previously been imposed on Lebanon.

The 1978 Camp David Accord between Israel and Egypt under American sponsorship was a "Black Swan" event for the Arab World. It meant a major and unprecedented geopolitical shift in the regional balance between the Arabs and Israel, even between the USSR and the United States. The Arabs lost the country that fought Israel; the burden was now on Syria. Being in Lebanon, or de facto controlling Lebanon, and to spoil this accord, Syria used whatever it had on hand to rectify the balance of power. Hence Kissinger's famous dictum: "No war without Egypt, no peace without Syria."[42]

During this new equation, the civil war returned to Lebanon until the Israeli invasion of 1982 thus starting another kind of conflict and war, with new regional dynamics especially after the Iranian Islamic revolution of 1979. The most important tectonic shift was the 1979 Iranian Islamic Revolution with Imam al Khomeini. This revolution shook the foundations of the Arab and Islamic world. It was an exclusive revolution per se, only for the Shia Twelver who follow the *wilayat al- faqih* doctrine—the guardianship of the jurist.[43] Whoever wanted to join were required to first be Shia, then twelver, and finally, believe in the guardianship of the jurist.

The seismic waves of this revolution rippled the whole region. It defied the Sunni Arab world; moreover, it revived a neo-imperialist tendency under the guise of Islam. The grand scheme of Islamic Iran in the region revived in Turkey the old enmity of the Ottomans and the Persians. Both old empires fought each other fiercely when the *Pax Mogolica* had ended after the withdrawal of the Mongols from the region. However, when the Pax Americana ended after the withdrawal of the U.S. forces from Iraq in 2011, both regional powers went back to trying to control the Fertile Crescent; as discussed earlier, Lebanon became a part of the Crescent.[44]

Therefore, 1979 and 1982 are two highly critical years for the modern history of Lebanon: 1979 led to the revival and rise of the Shia under the leadership of Iran, including the Lebanese ones; and the 1982 Israeli invasion led to the creation of the strategic relationship between Syria of Al Assad, and Iran of Al Khomeini. This invasion also led to the creation of the Lebanese Hezbollah party whose goal was to fight the Israeli occupation in Lebanon, and to remove the United States from the region. So the Shia of Lebanon were mobilized and drafted to be a part of the strategic axis of Iran and Syria; though the relationship between the Shia of Lebanon and those of Iran date back 500 years.[45] In addition, the Assad family owed the Shia of

Lebanon, especially the Imam Moussa Sadr, when the latter issued a fatwa in 1973 considering the Alawis of Syria as Shia Muslims, to facilitate the rule of Hafez Al Assad vis-à-vis the Sunni, especially the Muslim Brotherhood,[46] when drafting the Syrian constitution.

The 1982 invasion by the Israelis forces, in concordance with the Christian Lebanese militias, led to the destruction of the PLO as well as of the Lebanese infrastructure. This invasion ended for good the armed dimension of the Palestinians' resistance.

Lebanon in this turmoil did not change the historical course of choosing its political elites. The political solution was imposed again on Lebanon by the Israelis when they elected and lobbied in favor of the Christian militia leader, Bashir Gemayel.[47] Gemayel was assassinated by his brother, Amin, who followed as president of Lebanon. The Israelis withdrew to the security zone in southern Lebanon and the Syrians returned to Lebanon. Again, Lebanon will go through a lengthy period of instability where the leaderships have no influence at all on the main course of events.

In 1988, when the term of President Amine Gemayel ended with no possibility in sight to elect a new President or to renew or extend his term, he nominated an interim cabinet under the helm of General of the Lebanese Army, Michel Aoun. Aoun waged two destructive wars; the first against the Syrians under the slogan of the war of Liberation, the second against the leader of the Lebanese Forces Samir Geagea. Both wars were the straw that broke the camel's back of the Christian community in Lebanon, and changed the balance of power, tilting it toward the Muslims in all aspects. The war between Aoun and Geagea was a new phenomenon in the Lebanese equation of volatility and instability and a new dimension — that war could happen between people from the same sects.[48]

The civil war in Lebanon became futile and costly, and it was time to put an end to it, but how? To explain the process of ending the war, we go back to the Three Ring Model and the pattern. The United States gave the green light to end the war. Saudi Arabia as regional power, with the help of Morocco, Algeria, and Syria, created the political solution that was imposed by force via Syria on Lebanon—the Taef Agreement. From 1842 until 1990, nothing really changed in the bloody cycle of civil wars in Lebanon; history repeated itself but in different contexts, the circle and the arrow concept. Syria entered Lebanon by military force and ended the rule of Aoun and then took over Lebanon until 2005, when it was forced to withdraw from Lebanon under U.S. pressure after the assassination of Prime Minister Rafic Hariri.

The Lengthy Syrian Presence in Lebanon.

The Syrian hegemony over Lebanon was facilitated by an American green light, when the United States was preparing the campaign to liberate Kuwait from Saddam Hussein. It needed an Arab and Islamic cover for more legitimacy. The shrewd Assad exploited the opportunity, and sent Syrian forces to participate symbolically in the liberation of Kuwait; Lebanon was the big prize. Thus he achieved his geopolitical goal by only following the new rules of the game.

Lebanese Governance during the Syrian Regional Hegemony.[49]

The imposition of the Taef Agreement on Lebanon by the Syrian military force, in fact, validated our theory concerning the pattern in Lebanon—an imposed political solution. Moreover, it was a historical opportunity for President Hafez Al Assad to achieve his strategic goals, while the international and regional context favored taking over Lebanon for good. The Taef Agreement changed the internal balance of power among the sects. Instead of distributing political power along the ratio 6 to 1 as is done today, the distribution will be 50/50 percent. Moreover, the Maronite President lost most of his powers. According to former Defense Minister Albert Mansour,[50] the President of the Republic lost, with the Taef, almost all his powers; political, military, financial, and administrative. The president became powerless and instead of solving the Lebanese dilemma, the Taef agreement created more problems than solutions. The Taef agreement created a vital dilemma for the Christians. If they go along with the implementation, they lose; if they boycott it, they lose as well. The Christians oscillated between both courses of action.

Entering Lebanon by force and under a regional and international legitimacy was the most opportune time for Assad to complete his geopolitical design for Syria and his role in the region. After deciphering his plans in retrospect vis-à-vis Lebanon, Assad's calculations were based on the most important geopolitical equation, which is:

- Lebanon is indispensible for Syria, it is the vital strategic depth for Syria.
- Lebanon is also the soft belly of Syria, the ills of Syria could come from Lebanon.
- Lebanon, under the Syrian thumb, gives Syria a major global and regional status; without Lebanon, Syria is just an ordinary regional country in the Fertile Crescent.

- If Syria loses Lebanon, the struggle will be on her soul,[51] on how to control Syria; it will be the main stake in the region, on one hand; on the other, if Syria has Lebanon, it will lead the struggle in the region beyond its borders, and will be the linchpin of the Fertile Crescent.
- Lebanon can add to Syria the most important tools needed for a grand design in the region, among many, the political, and financial, as well as the media one.

The Taef agreement was presented to Assad on a golden plate. It was the historical opportunity to complete his design without being interrupted, neither by the Arabs nor the United States, and not by Israel. He became a necessity for them after he repositioned himself and followed the tides of change after the fall of his main sponsor, the USSR. This was the macro level of Assad's design for Lebanon. It denotes how shrewd he was, and how he had in depth knowledge and a sense of history; and how he was able to relate the macro to the micro practically. It also denotes how patient he was by following the famous dictum of *Muawiyah*:

> I never apply the sword when the lash suffices, nor the lash when my tongue is enough. If there is even one thread binding me to my fellow man, I do not let it break. If he pulls, I loosen. If he loosens, I pull.[52]

Assad, the Muawiyah of the 20th century, governed Lebanon at the micro level by suppressing the Sunni, especially Hariri, knowing in advance that Hariri was the man of Saudi Arabia in Lebanon, pro-American, and a close friend to French President Jacques Chirac. All the above hindered his design for Lebanon.

To get rid of his main historical opponents in Lebanon, the Christian Maronites, he exiled some, imprisoned others, and got the services of the rest by intimidation.[53] In fact, the Maronites were the main hurdle for Assad, since they considered themselves as the creators of Greater Lebanon. Aoun was exiled to France, as was former President Gemayel. The leader of the Lebanese Forces, a staunch supporter of the Taef Agreement, was jailed for almost 11 years. The Christians of Lebanon were leaderless for almost 14 years, while Taef deprived them of their main historical role in the governance; a new kind of leadership ensued under the control of the Syrian influence—in the Christian realm, the leaders were called the puppets of the Syrians. Last, but not least, the Syrian regime opened up the whole state of Lebanon for the Shia Amal movement, the most important party of Hezbollah. Hezbollah is considered the offspring of the strategic relationship between Assad and Khomeini; it is the military arm to project power in multidimensions.

When the militias of Lebanon were disarmed after the Taef agreement, Hezbollah kept its arsenal under the slogan of Islamic resistance to liberate the occupied land by Israel after the 1982 invasion. The resistance was exclusive for the party of God; the other secular parties were denied by force the sacred role of fighting the occupier, keeping in mind that the first resistant shot fired on the Israeli in Lebanon was pure secular. It is worth noting that Hezbollah, with President Assad, the father, was a controlled tool for his regional design. He never personally met the Secretary of the party of God, and the relationship between Iran and Hezbollah had to go through Syria first for the final decision—this changed dramatically with Assad, the son.

For instance, the Iranian government was against the Taef Agreement, as it marginalized the Shia of Lebanon. To spoil the situation, the Iranian ambassador to Syria crossed the border to Lebanon to meet the leaders of Hezbollah, asking them to oppose the implementation of Taef. President Assad was aware of the Iranian design, stood firm, and ignored the Iranians wishes.[54] From the macro to the micro level, the Syrians, through their Lebanese puppets, tightly controlled Lebanon.[55] The security apparatus were under the total Syrian control — Army, Iraqi Security Force, and so on — as well as the political institutions, elections, assignments, etc. The foreign policy of Lebanon had to be geared by the Syrians to serve their grand strategy design.

In this period, we could say that the absence of volatility and instability was at the expense of the liberty and sovereignty of Lebanon. Even, the leadership was assigned from top to bottom — it was a stiff and tough micromanagement. For instance, Sunni Leader Hariri, the architect of the Taef, was a billionaire and considered the man of Saudi Arabia in Lebanon. The Maronites had no sponsor at that period in time, since their role became irrelevant in linking between East and the West; but they were a major factor of the problem, or rather the main problem, but not necessarily a part of the solution. As far as the Shia factions were concerned, they were the main proxies of Syria and Iran. Hence, the stability of Lebanon in that critical period of time was not the by-product of the Lebanese leaderships, rather it still depended on the dynamics of the geopolitical games in the region and on the whims of the regional powers.

To be more precise, there was a tight Syrian system of control on all levels, as mentioned earlier. This was institutionalized, and it had a structure and a *modus operandi*. For instance, the main intelligence bureau was located in the Bekaa Valley in the town of Anjar. The regional intelligence bureau was located there and in each administrative district—hub and periphery. The main bureau was responsible for all day-to-day affairs in Lebanon from security issues to elections at all levels, even to economy. The passage to Damascus had to go through the main gate, which was Anjar, except for privileged people and high-ranking officials. Even at the highest level of leadership, it is extremely embarrassing to discuss how, for instance, the president of Lebanon was chosen, elected, and how his term extended.[56] As defunct Lebanese president Elias Hraoui stated:

> In 1995 on the 15th of April, I met with President Assad for more than 5 hours. He said to me that the region is going through a critical time, and change at the leadership level is not a good option. And since we are in an excellent relationship, I suggest that you extend your term for 3 more years.[57]

Hraoui continues:

> ... The Speaker of the House, Nabih Birri, was assigned by Damascus to prepare the Parliament to amend the constitution. . . .[58]

The trigger for the whole process above, to start, was not made in Lebanon. The President continues:

> On the 11th of October 1995, the Egyptian newspaper *Al-Ahram* published an interview with President

Assad, saying, that the Lebanese have agreed to extend the term of the President.[59]

While being President for more than 9 years, and knowing tacitly that Assad preferred General of the Lebanese Army Emile Lahoud to be the next President of Lebanon, Hraoui, while on the road from Damascus to Beirut, called Lahoud and congratulated him for being chosen as next President of Lebanon. Afterward, the charade continued within the legal institutions.[60]

Points in analyzing the Lebanese status during this period, according to the Three Ring Model, are:

- At the international level, the United States was in Iraq, with two no-fly zones. The Lebanese question was geopolitically irrelevant. Russia, after the fall of the USSR, was immersed internally by a high degree of instability.
- At the regional level, the sponsors of the Taef Agreement gave up on their role for Lebanon, especially the Gulf States, for fear of the situation from the encircled Iraq, and the looming danger of the Iranian revolution.
- Locally, Lebanon is left to the Syrian unchallenged hegemony.[61] Thus, Lebanon became the means for Assad to achieve his regional goals.

In June 2000, Assad died from a heart attack. His son, Bashar, was elected after being prepared for this contingency for more than 5 years. Changes in Syria are directly reflected in Lebanon. Whether by intimidation or choice, accordingly, the system of control in Lebanon was changed, upgraded to suit the new realities. The Israeli withdrawal from southern Lebanon on May 24, 2000, after 18 years of occupation and insurgency by Hezbollah—backed by Iran and Syria—

created new rules for new kinds of games. Simply said internal strife resurfaced. The issue of Hezbollah's arms was brought up. The Syrian presence in Lebanon was put to the question. The relevance of the strategic axis of Iran, Syria, and Hezbollah was contented post liberation.

The most important declaration dealing with these major issues came from the Maronite Bishops.[62] This declaration defied the Syrian presence, asking for their withdrawal and even blaming them for most of the Lebanese ills. This led back to internal strife. To legitimize the arms of Hezbollah after the Liberation of the South, a *casus belli* was designed in Shebaa Farms, as an occupied territory by Israel that needed to be liberated.

The greatest "Black Swan" event of the 21st century occurred on September 11, 2001. The global war on terror of the American President George W. Bush was focused on the Middle East as the main theater, especially the Arab world, since 15 of the 19 culprits were Saudis, one was Lebanese, one was Egyptian, and two were from the United Arab Emirates. After the war on Afghanistan in 2001, Iraq was occupied in 2003 and Saddam Hussein was toppled.

Using the Three Ring Model, the geopolitical shift in the world and the region was unprecedented. How? The global ring was dominated by the United States; it was its Unipolar Moment,[63] never been experienced in the history of great powers.[64] The Russians reassured the Americans that they were in the same fight against terrorism, and *Le Monde*, the famous French Newspaper, wrote in its opening, "Nous sommes tous Americains" ("We are all Americans").[65]

In 2003, the major shift was the occupation of Iraq and the toppling of Saddam Hussein. Thus, the international ring coalesced tightly with the regional ring. Because of the disparity of power between both rings, the ripples were felt all over the region. The analogy of the United States resembling a 5,000-pound gorilla entering a gift shop; however it moved, the consequences were very high. Iraq was the center of gravity of the region; from this center, the United States could project power and influence in the whole region. But the American designs were of an utopist nature in a region where history weighed heavily. The Iraqi adventure was supposed to be a short and quick battle in a long war; it turned out to be the main U.S. battle. The Syrians, as well as the Iranians, refused to cooperate to help stabilize Iraq post Saddam. How could they help, knowing that their turn could be next? It was also a historical occasion to bleed the United States, remove it, and dominate the region. On the local ring, Syria held Lebanon tight for many geopolitical imperatives discussed earlier, and Hezbollah later dominated the Lebanese scene.

In 2004, the United Nations Security Council (UNSC) issued Resolution 1559, asking for the Syrian withdrawal from Lebanon and the election of a new president when Lahoud's term ended.[66] Resolution 1559 was the offspring of cooperation between Bush and Chirac. Since Hariri was a close friend of Chirac, he was accused indirectly as being the father of this resolution. On February 14, 2005, Hariri was assassinated by a huge car bomb in the middle of Beirut. According to many analysts, Hariri was killed for the future roles he might have played, not on what he had done. He was caught in a very big regional and global game where the stakes were very high, and he paid the price. He was assassinated, not because he was a Sunni, rather because he was the man of the Kingdom of Saudi Arabia in Lebanon in a time when the regional rivalry among regional great powers was at its peak.

This assassination was the main reason for Syria to withdraw its military forces from Lebanon, though not its intelligence, influence, and apparatus. When pressure was put on Assad, he acquiesced, however he promised to destroy Lebanon. In fact, Lebanon sunk into the abyss of violence and political assassinations. Then Lebanon was divided into two camps: 14th March and 8th March. Though both groups were multisectarian, the game was played between them on zero sum logic. On the one hand, the 14th of March were backed by Saudi Arabia regionally, and by the United States on the international level. On the other, the 8th of March were backed regionally by Iran and Syria and internationally by Russia through Iran. An international tribunal[67] was created under Chapter 7 of the UN Charter since the Lebanese Government was not able to convene and decide this issue. This tribunal was seen by March 8th as a tool of the imperial world, specifically the United States, to punish Hezbollah for being a part of the axis of resistance.

After the assassination of Hariri, Syria was considered the main culprit by the 14th of March group, based on some threats that were made to Hariri directly by the Syrian President.[68] In fact, the tribunal later issued its indictment, accusing members of Hezbollah as the main culprits for the assassination of Hariri. Hezbollah denied any responsibility, refusing to hand over the accused members, and Lebanon entered a new round of volatility and instability where sectarianism was high, especially between Sunni and Shia.

During this period, the leadership was powerless in how to stabilize Lebanon. What really created the negative momentum of instability were the dynamic and the clash between the international ring and the regional one. Do not forget that the United States was still in Iraq, with Bush at the helm of the U.S. administration and his grand design for the new Middle East.

In this realm, the role of Lebanese leadership from all factions was minimal, limited, and at the whim of the bigger players, whether regional or international. Here we go back to our theory and prove its relevancy again; the stability of Lebanon was not yet in the hands of its leadership. In order to assuage and deflate the tense situation in Lebanon, Speaker of the House Nabih Birri convened the leaders of the constituencies of the Lebanese sectarian map. Good intentions were shown from all parties, as if there were no connections between what was in Lebanon and what was happening in the region.

On July 12, 2006, the sixth Arab-Israeli war started; not between Israel and the Arab states, rather it was between a nonstate actor Hezbollah against the strongest, most advanced army in the Middle East, the Israeli Defense Force—considered a postmodern army. Without going into the complex analysis and characteristics of this war, we could say the following: Israel lost because it did not win. Hezbollah won because it did not lose. Israel was shocked, surprised, and found itself ill-prepared for this kind of war, a hybrid between asymmetric and conventional.[69] Israel was not able to measure its success against a shadowy enemy. Although Israel bombed and destroyed a bank of targets, how was it to relate this war to politics? Especially after Israel reached an impasse on how to terminate the war when the war started to follow the law of diminishing returns. Hezbollah got stronger, as well as Iran and Syria. The political ramifications were huge and altered Bush's project and vision for the new Middle East.

At the beginning of the war, Hezbollah was accused by some Arab countries, Sunni mainly, and the Arab League as dragging Lebanon to unnecessary war.[70] After the tide of war started to tilt toward Hezbollah, the Arab league changed its stance by supporting Hezbollah against Israel. This attitude never deceived Hezbollah on the real intentions of the Arab Sunni states vis-à-vis Hezbollah or Iran and Syria. Hezbollah was praised in the Arab and Islamic world as the only entity, not even a state, that was able to stand firm against Israel and maybe even defeat it. We could see, for instance, posters of Sayyed Hassan Nasrallah, secretary general of Hezbollah, hung all over the streets of Cairo. The streets of the Arab world transcended the fact that Nasrallah is a Shia, and focused on the achievement against Israel.

This sensation, however, was not really felt in Lebanon. The war did not change the stance of Hezbollah's opposition, and it was accused of deceiving the Lebanese by promising not to wage war, but actually violating its promise. Even Nasrallah himself said during a TV interview, "we would not have snatched soldiers if we thought it would spark a war."[71] Moreover, the 14th of March faction accused Hezbollah of costing Lebanon more than U.S.$4 billion.

The reconstruction of Lebanon after the war of 2006 also followed our Three Ring Model theory, as far as the financial aids that were given to Lebanon. The regional players fought each other in Lebanon; Lebanon was destroyed in this fight. The same regional players poured their money to rebuild the damage that their war caused to Lebanon. Hezbollah tagged this war as a divine victory.[72] Israel tagged it as the Second Lebanese war; the first was in 1982. The UNSC Resolution 1701 implemented the cessation of hostilities, and added the United Nations Interim Force in Lebanon (UNIFIL) in the role of a buffer between Israel and Hezbollah.

The straw that broke the camel's back between the Lebanese factions, and endangered the cohabitation, was the semi-civil war of May 7, 2008, if the July's war was considered the culminating point for Hezbollah as far as war is concerned. It is also considered the maximum point of maturity for the party of God; Hezbollah's dilemma was, what to do after defeating, or denying, Israel the victory? What to do with this excess of power?

On May 7, Hezbollah invaded Beirut and on May 6, the Lebanese Government considered Hezbollah's communication network as a direct violation of the state's sovereignty.[73] This Weberian[74] approach of the Lebanese government at that time was a matter of life and death for Hezbollah. Hezbollah could not endanger its military operations by using the official networks of the state against the most advanced country in the world in electronics, eavesdropping, and cyber warfare. Hence the invasion of Beirut by Hezbollah and its proxies under the Slogan: "the arms to protect the arms." It was a dangerous deviation by Hezbollah of how and where to use the arms of resistance; however, Nasrallah created the necessary mental formula, rationale, and justification for his act, at least for his group and allies.[75] In fact, Hezbollah, due to the huge disparity and excess of power that it held vis-à-vis other factions internally, invaded Beirut on May 7, 2008. This super quick victory in urban Beirut proved that Hezbollah had been preparing for all possible contingencies concerning its operational security.

Whether it was a miscalculation or an intended decision by the government—maybe both—to disable Hezbollah, this decision had proven to be a precarious situation for Lebanon. Moreover, it showed the grand design of Hezbollah for Lebanon, and its role in the regional struggle for primacy. In addition, it exposed the weak points of Hezbollah, especially within its military design. The 7th of May mini-sectarian war unearthed the fault lines among the sects in Lebanon, mainly between Shia and Sunni, given the fact that Beirut historically is considered the capital of the Sunni. Hezbollah was demonized regionally by the Arab-Sunni street, though Nasrallah hailed May 7th as a glorious day.[76]

The Christian leadership of Lebanon were spectators on the 7th of May war, though divided between 14th and 8th of March factions. The main battle, whether directly or indirectly, was between Sunni and Druze on the one side and Hezbollah on the other. The 7th of May did not deviate from the pattern of the Lebanese politics, after each civil war regardless of its context and dynamics, an imposed political solution had to be reached. The Doha agreement was the imposed political solution on Lebanon and the main points in this agreement were:[77]

- The parliament will convene to elect the agreed-upon candidate, General Michel Sleiman, as the new Lebanese President.
- A government of national unity to be formed with 30 ministers, 16 to the majority, 11 to the opposition, and 3 for the president. All parties pledge by virtue of this Agreement not to resign or obstruct the work of the Government.

- In accordance with the electoral law of 1960, the district (qada') will be adopted as the electoral constituency in Lebanon.

This imposed political solution gave Lebanon a leeway from instability and volatility for a short period of time. It was a tactical calculation by the Lebanese factions, as well as by the regional players, to acquiesce to Doha agreement. Said differently, it was a battle within a fierce long war that is still raging where every party prepares for the next round. This next round took place in Syria after the so-called Arab Spring hit the foundations of the Middle East regional order, especially the Arab world.

THE ARAB SPRING SYNDROME

If the fall of the Ottoman Empire and the partition of the region according to the Sykes Picot[78] secret agreement in 1916, and the Arab revolution against it, are considered the most important Arab Black Swan events at the beginning of the 20th century because of the creation of the Arab nation-states, we could say that the so-called Arab Spring is so far the most devastating Black Swan event in the 21st century for the Arab world.

In the first Black Swan event, the Arab nation-states were created, though at the expense of the Ottoman Empire, which was considered the Islamic Khilafa. The new nation-state transcended the micro divisions at the religious, sectarian, tribal, and ethnic levels. The Arab Spring Black Swan event had undone the first one, as we say in the computer parlance. A new sample of an Arab state started to develop. In a gaze from above into the region, we can notice the following after almost 3 years of this earthquake:

- The fall of the state; there are governments but no governance.
- The new-old player is political Islam with different platforms: the Muslim brotherhood, the Jihadist, Wahhabis, Justice and Development Party (AKP) in Turkey, and so on.
- No modifications on the state's recognized borders, and no partition as well; the fault lines are again as before, the religious, sectarian, tribal, and ethnic — Yemen, Libya, Iraq, and Lebanon, just to mention a few.
- The volatility in the new format of the Arab state is very high, depending on the constituencies of each country.

During the first event, the nation states were created and, although we fought for union and for borders, this creation transcended the religious, sectarian, and tribal fault lines. When the Arab Spring hit Syria on March 15, 2011, we could say that the rules of the geopolitical game for Lebanon were altered for good. The regional ring followed a new dynamic, highly dangerous for Syria and Lebanon. The local ring followed an unprecedented hectic behavior; the level of uncertainties reached its highest peak. In this new dynamic, some of the old historical paradigms that used to govern the relationship between Lebanon and Syria, whether in peace or conflict and war, broke up for good. Old players were no more efficient; new ones emerged.

Analyzing Lebanon's Status Following the Three Ring Model.

During the 1975 Lebanese civil war, the geopolitical earthquake hit Lebanon hard. The dynamics of the Three Ring Model canalized the currents of change into Lebanon, the weakest point in the region, due to the presence of the PLO, and after the October war between Arabs and Israel, lead to a serious energy crisis for the West. In 2011, the United States withdrew its forces from Iraq permanently, even without reaching an adequate agreement with the Iraqi government. This withdrawal created a geopolitical vacuum in the region that had to be filled.

In this instance, Iran was ready for regional hegemony, due to its grand strategy that includes Iraq, Syria, Lebanon, and even the Gaza strip where Hamas is located. The linchpin and the center of gravity of the Iranian grand strategy is Syria par excellence. Iran with Syria is a regional hegemony; Iran without Syria is limited at its best to southern Iraq where the Shia twelver are the majority, thus creating a buffer for Iran. So the grand design to deny Iran the regional hegemony would be as the prominent strategic Chinese thinker Sun Tzu said "to attack the strategy" of Iran indirectly.[79] The two main important means for Iran to achieve its regional hegemony are Syria and Hezbollah in Lebanon. In the July 2006 war, Hezbollah survived the Israeli might. In 2011, Syria is where the geopolitical earthquake is passing.

This regional jockeying for primacy was triggered by the U.S. withdrawal from Iraq as said earlier; this withdrawal has revived among the regional great powers the security dilemma, since this withdrawal gave Iran an unprecedented opportunity to fill the geopolitical vacuum due to its huge influence in the Fertile Crescent, from Iraq to Gaza, through Syria and Lebanon.

When the Syrian regime started to lose ground inside Syria, Iran had to interfere through Hezbollah's military. The culminating point was the battle of Al-Qusair in Syria where Hezbollah was the defining factor in the victory of the Syrian regime; though the Lebanese government adapted the policy of noninterference vis-à-vis the Syrian crisis. The new slogan for Hezbollah to interfere militarily in Syria is to protect the resistance, and foil the conspiracy of the West, mainly the United States and Israel.[80] The geopolitical goals of Hezbollah for interfering in Syria are:

- To protect some Shia villages inside Syria, as well as some Shia sacred Shrines.
- To create a buffer space inside Syria to protect the main Shia villages and cities inside Lebanon, of which are along the Lebanese-Syrian borders. Thus the routes for jihadists will be blocked toward Lebanon.[81]
- Al-Qusair is highly important strategically for the regime in Syria as well; it is the backyard that protects the capital Damascus. It is the strategic link between the capital and the coastal area of Syria where the majority of the Alawis reside.
- The presence of Hezbollah in this area blocked the routes for jihadists, and denied them any access to Syria, whether to fight along the rebels or smuggle weapons.
- Last, but not least, is the Iranian decision to fight in Syria via Hezbollah under the slogan, one for all, and all for one; referring to the tri-

partite summit in Syria in 2010 between Assad, Ahmadinejad, and Hassan Nasrallah. The main absentee was the Lebanese President, though Lebanon as a country was the main dish on the table.

Paradigm Shift.

Hezbollah's interference in Syria is unique. It marks the first time that a Lebanese faction fought in Syria; even holding territory with the acquiescence of its government. It is the first time for Lebanon to be a secured soft belly for Syria, instead of historically being the weakest point. It is the first time that Syria is volatile, the Golan Heights are unstable, and yet southern Lebanon is stable. In this major paradigm shift, Lebanon is forced by the regional and international dynamics to be carried by the flow. Hezbollah has two agendas, local and regional. The primary objective of the two is the regional agenda. Thus, the Lebanese policy of noninterference toward Syria is irrelevant for the party of God. Lebanese factions see Hezbollah interference in Syria as a sectarian war, though the geopolitical game is the main issue.

All of the discussion previously mentioned is putting Lebanon into a precarious situation, where the future of Lebanon is at stake. Even the leadership of all factions is powerless in this situation, due to its complexities, and the lack of means to influence. In Lebanon, we can say "Who is capable is not willing, who is willing is not capable." Even if Hezbollah is capable, they are not willing. The willing are the 14th of March faction, but they are not capable. Thus, Lebanon is going through the same pattern of internal strife that may lead to a new kind of civil war, even though

Hassan Nasrallah suggested that the Lebanese could fight each other in Syria, just not in Lebanon.[82] This could be a new paradigm shift, as Syria is the buffer zone, the battle ground for the Lebanese to settle their accounts instead of vice versa.

The Lebanese dilemma today is the Syrian catastrophe. What kind of Syria will emerge after the civil war? Will it be religious or secular? How will the power in Syria be redistributed? What would the role of minorities be? What would be the implications on Lebanon? Will Syria mirror the Lebanese situation, divided along sectarian lines? How will the consequences unfold in Lebanon in case of the defeat, or the victory of the regime, and as well as Hezbollah? What would be the implications on Lebanon, if Syria turned to be a de facto partitioned country? (See Map 5-5.)

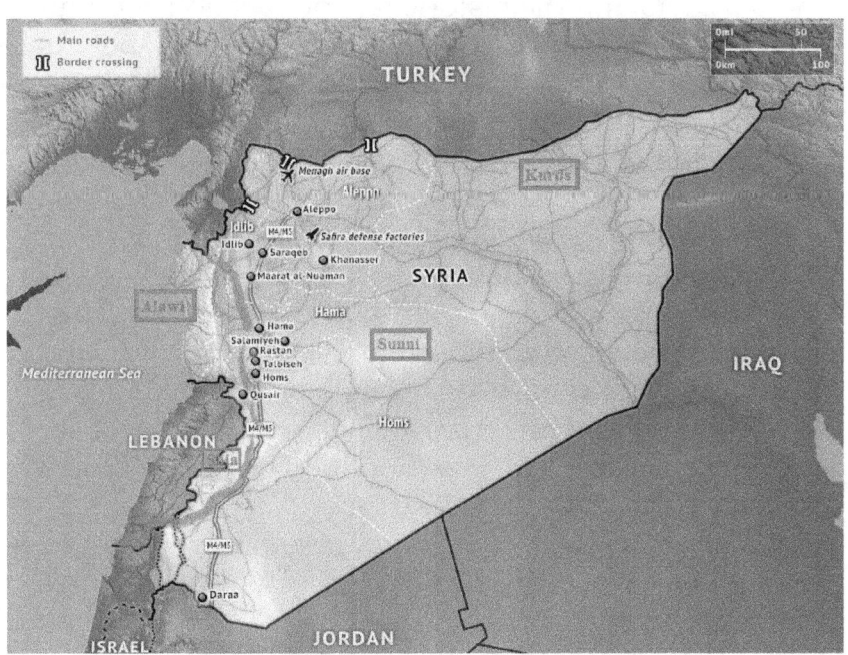

Map 5-5. A De Facto Partitioned Syria.

CONCLUSION

In this chapter, we discussed the role of leadership in a Lebanon that swings between volatility and quasi-stability. We proved that the theory of the Three Ring Model and the pattern is still relevant to analyze the case of the Land of the Cedars — Lebanon. The case of Lebanon never really changed in its essence; the circle and the arrow concept is still applicable since Lebanon is still in the same geographical location, the Fertile Crescent, where old games keep reemerging, but in a different morphology.

Since its inception as an idea starting from 1842 until today, Lebanon is a volatile country due to many factors, geographical, political as well as cultural. The Three Ring Model applied at the macro level will help understand the historic fate of Lebanon and perhaps predict the future. However, this does not relieve us from going deep in the micro level to get the holistic picture.

But the question still is: Can we escape this fate in Lebanon? Should we repeat permanently the Sisyphus's task? Are we doomed? Should we surrender to the negative dynamics of the Three Ring Model? Is democracy for Lebanon a killer? Are we doomed to choose between authoritarianism, occupation, and democracy? These are the questions constantly posed to me by my students from all factions and sects. Usually my answer is also based on the Three Ring Model and the pattern discussed earlier.

When civil war occurs in Lebanon followed by an imposed political solution, it means that the three rings of our theory are in sync, not clashing. During this historical moment, the Lebanese elites from all factions, religions, and sects should take the opportunity to counter the myth of Sisyphus and try to create a political platform to buffer Lebanon from all the ills of the region and the global order. Unfortunately, these elites are taken prisoners by their own will, and sink into the whirlpool and the dynamics of the Three Ring Model. Thus, Lebanon will oscillate for the foreseeable future between volatility and quasi-stability, but always in favor of instability and a high risk of being swollen into civil war again and again. May God protect and save the land, the Land of the Cedars.

ENDNOTES - CHAPTER 5

1. See *www.merriam-webster.com/dictionary/geopolitics*.

2. See *mapsofwar.com/ind/imperial-history.html*. I suggest to visit this site and play the video in focusing on the location of Lebanon as the main geographical intersection of all old empires that invaded the region. Unfortunately, they are still relevant today.

3. Alvin Toeffler, *The Third Wave*, New York: Bantam, May 1, 1984.

4. The map is available from *www.bible-history.com* as modified by the writer to clarify the idea of the Fertile Crescent.

5. This theory is developed by the writer while teaching at university level, the course "History of Lebanon and the Middle East," also while teaching Geopolitics, especially the Case study of Lebanon.

6. Richard N. Haass, *The Age of Nonpolarity, What Will Follow U.S. Dominance*, available from *www.foreignaffairs.com/articles/63397/richard-n-haass/the-age-of-nonpolarity*.

7. Saad Eddin Ibrahim, *The 'New Middle East' Bush Is Resisting*, available from *www.washingtonpost.com/wp-dyn/content/article/2006/08/22/AR2006082200978_pf.html*.

8. As it happened on May 7, 2008, in Beirut and Mount Lebanon, between mainly Hezbollah Amal Movement from one side; and Future Movement and the Druze of Walid Jumblat on the other side. It was a mini-civil war with different aspects from the previous civil wars, however. The Doha agreement is considered as an imposed political solution and led to the election of the President and to the parliamentary elections.

9. See *www.exploringgeopolitics.org/Interview_Flint_Colin_Structure_Agency_Identity_Peace_Networks_Geopolitical_Codes_Visions_Agents_Actors_Representations_Practices_Spaces_Powers_Environmental_Geopolitics.html*.

10. In the current government, as well as the previous one, all we have in the statement that deals with the national security strategy is the triad of the people, the army and the resistance, meaning Hezbollah, where Hezbollah is the strongest and calling the shots all the time.

11. In 2010, the remittances to Lebanon amounted to U.S. $8,406 million, available from *www.migrationinformation.org/datahub/remittances/Lebanon.pdf*.

12. Riad Kobaissi, from Michel Chiha to Rafik Hariri: Continuity and Discontinuity in the Process of "Lebanonization," available from *https://ecommons.lau.edu.lb:8443/xmlui/bitstream/handle/10725/1155/Riad_Kobaissi_Thesis.pdf?sequence=1*.

13. Arend Lijphart, "Consociational Democracy," *World Politics*, Vol. 21, No. 2, January 1969, pp. 207-225.

14. T. David Mason, *Sustaining The Peace After Civil War*, Carlisle, PA: Strategic Studies Institute, U.S. Army War College, December 2007, p. 45, available from *www.strategicstudiesinstitute.army.mil/pubs/display.cfm?pubID=819*.

15. Kamal Salibi, *The Modern History of Lebanon*, Westport, CT: Praeger, September 30, 1976.

16. The source of the map is available from *publishing.cdlib. org/ucpressebooks/view?docId=ft6199p06t&chunk.id=d0e1095&toc. id=&brand=ucpress.*

17. The 12 members include four Maronites, three Druses, two Greek Orthodox, one Catholic, one Shia, and one Sunni.

18. Cited by Ghenwa Hayek, *Dislocations: Space, Nation, and Identity in Lebanese Fiction, 1970-2003,* Providence, RI: Brown University, 2011, p. 24, available from *https://repository.library.brown. edu/fedora/objects/bdr:11196/datastreams/PDF/content.*

19. *Ibid.*

20. Especially the Maronite Patriarch Elias Howayek, available from *www.matnfiles.com/news_details.php?id=3304.*

21. *History of Lebanon, Switzerland of the East* (1943 AD— 1969 AD), available from *www.lgic.org/en/history_lebanon19 43.php;* or *www.britannica.com/EBchecked/topic/1380862/Lebanese-National-Pact.*

22. Nassim Nicholas Taleb, "What is a 'Black Swan'?" available from *www.youtube.com/watch?v=BDbuJtAiABA.*

23. Farid El-Khazen, "Permanent Settlement of Palestinians in Lebanon: A Recipe for Conflict," *Journal of Refugee Studies,* Vol. 10, No. 3, 1997, available from *almashriq.hiof.no/ddc/projects/pspa/ khazen.html.*

24. Approximately 150,000 refugees came to Lebanon, available from *www.lgic.org/en/history_lebanon1943.php.*

25. In the Eisenhower Doctrine (January 5, 1957), the Cold War period after World War II, U.S. foreign-policy pronouncement by President Dwight D. Eisenhower promised military or economic aid to any Middle Eastern country needing help in resisting communist aggression, available from *www.britannica.com/ EBchecked/topic/181513/Eisenhower-Doctrine.*

26. Nicholas Nassif, *Al Riasaa Al Lubbnaniah fi Mahab al Reeh*, (The Lebanese Leadership Is Exposed to Storms), Beiruit, Lebanon: Issam Fares Center for the Lebanese Affairs, 2007, p. 20.

27. It is told that U.S. Ambassador Robert D. Murphy was assigned to negotiate the election of Fouad Chehab. When he visited Raymond Eddeh, a prominent Lebanese politician, to tell him about the deal, Eddeh refused and presented his candidacy for the presidency under the slogan that Lebanon is democratic, an interview with Nicholas Nassif, a writer and journalist.

28. El-Khazen.

29. Nassif, p. 14.

30. *The 3 "Nos" of Khartoum*, available from *www.sixdaywar. org/content/khartoum.asp*.

31. *What was the 1969 Cairo Agreement between Lebanon and the PLO?* available from *www.palestinefacts.org/pf_1967to1991_lebanon _cairo_1969.php*.

32. It is said that the General of the Army at that time, Emile El-Bustani, who was heading the Lebanese delegation to Cairo, agreed on the agreement after it was promised he would be the next Lebanese President. Even this agreement was ratified by the Lebanese Parliament without being read and debated publicly. The Cairo agreement was annulled by President Amin Gemayel in 1982 after the PLO was routed out of Lebanon after the Israeli invasion.

33. Roger J. Azzam, *Liban l'instruction d'un crime: 30 Ans de guerre* (Lebanon to Investigate a Crime: 30 Years of War), Cheminements (Pathways), October 1, 2005.

34. Mentioned in Michele Steinberg, *Kissinger Plan for Lebanon: Death by 'Democracy'*, available from *www.larouchepub.com/ eiw/public/2005/2005_20-29/2005_20-29/2005-21/pdf/41-42_21_ int.pdf*.

35. Region in the suburb of Beirut consisting of mostly Christians.

36. Is it a conspiracy theory approach? Maybe, personally, I do not take it seriously, however, the dynamics of the geopolitical game at that time made Lebanon the killing zone of the region, as is Syria today.

37. As'ad AbuKhalil, *Hafez Al-Assad in 1976*, available from *english.al-akhbar.com/node/8733*.

38. Map of Lebanon during the civil war of 1975, available from *www.pbs.org*.

39. AbuKhalil.

40. Hafez Asaad Speech, available from *www.youtube.com/watch?v=bdckwk_bNgY*.

41. *Lebanon — The Riyadh Conference and the Arab Deterrent Force*, available from *www.mongabay.com/history/lebanon/lebanon-the_riyadh_conference_and_the_arab_deterrent_force.html*.

42. Cited in Michael J. Totten, "Contentions No Peace without Syria," *Commentary Magazine*, 2009, available from *www.commentarymagazine.com/2009/08/31/no-peace-without-syria/*.

43. What is *Wilayat al-Faqih*? See *www.al-islam.org/shiapolitical-thought/3.htm*.

44. Soner Cagaptay and Tyler Evans, "Balancing Iran," *The American Interest Magazine*, September-October 2013, available from *www.the-american-interest.com/article.cfm?piece=1469*.

45. H. E. Chehabi, Houchang Chehabi, ed., *Distant Relations: Iran and Lebanon in the Last 500 Years*, London, UK: I. B. Tauris, April 3, 2007.

46. Fouad Ajami, *The Vanished Imam: Musa al Sadr and the Shia of Lebanon*, Ithaca, NY: Cornell University Press, August 25, 1987, p. 174.

47. Benni Morris, *Righteous Victims: A History of the Zionist-Arab Conflict, 1881-2001*, Updated Ed., Westminster, MD: Vintage, August 28, 2001, especially the chapter dealing with the 1982 invasion. I was in the military academy during the election of Gemayel; the only deputy who really defied this election is a Christian Greek orthodox named Albert Moukhaiber.

48. The same fighting happened between Hezbollah and Amal movement in the South and in Beirut. Both are Shia twelver.

49. Unpublished paper presented to the Center of Future Strategic Studies in Cairo, Egypt, 2006.

50. Albert Mansour, *Al Inquilad Ala al Taef*, Jeddah, Saudi Arabia: Dar Al Jadid, 1993.

51. Patrick Seale, *The Struggle for Syria*, New Haven, CT: Yale University Press, September 10, 1987, especially the Foreword of Albert Hourani.

52. Bryan Caplan, *Social Intelligence: The Wisdom of Muawiya*, available from *econlog.econlib.org/archives/2012/11/social_intellig.html*.

53. Marius Deeb, *Syria's Terrorist War on Lebanon and the Peace Process*, Basingstoke, Hampshire, UK: Palgrave/Macmillan, June 12, 2003.

54. Jubin M. Goodarzi, *Syria and Iran: Diplomatic Alliance and Power Politics in the Middle East*, London, UK: I. B. Tauris, July 7, 2009.

55. William Harris, "Twilight Lebanon, 1990-2011," *Middle East Review of International Affairs*, Vol. 17, No. 1, Spring 2013, available from *www.gloria-center.org/2013/03/twilight-lebanon-1990-2011/*.

56. The term of the Lebanese President is only 6 years, could be renewed or extended only through amending the constitution.

57. Camille Mnassa and Elias Hraoui, *"Awdat Al Joumhouriat min al douwailat ila al dawla,"* ("Return of the Republic from Statelets to State"), *Dar Annahar*, Beiruit, Lebanon, 2002, p. 402.

58. *Ibid.*, p. 403.

59. *Ibid.*, p. 405.

60. *Ibid.*, pp. 604-605.

61. Harris.

62. Declaration of the Maronite Bishops, September 20, 2000, available from *www.oocities.org/capitolhill/parliament/2587/declaration.html*.

63. Charles Krauthammer, "The Unipolar Moment," *Foreign Affairs*, available from *www.foreignaffairs.com/articles/46271/charles-krauthammer/the-unipolar-moment*.

64. "The former French Foreign Minister tagged USA after the fall of USSR as a Hyper-power," *The New York Times*, 1999, available from *www.nytimes.com/1999/02/05/news/05iht-france.t_0.html?pagewanted=print*.

65. Jean-Marie Colombani, *Nous sommes tous Américains* (We Are All Americans), available from *www.lemonde.fr/idees/article/2007/05/23/nous-sommes-tous-americains_913706_3232.html*.

66. Resolution 1559, 2004, available from *www.un.org/News/Press/docs/2004/sc8181.doc.htm*.

67. Special Tribunal for Lebanon, UNSCR 1757, available from *www.stl-tsl.org/en/*.

68. An op-ed written by Ahmad Al Jarallah in the Kuwaiti newspaper, *Alsiyasa*, available from *www.aramaic-dem.org/Arabic/Archev/AL_Seyassah/37.htm*.

69. For more details, read Elias Hanna, "Lessons Learned from the Recent War in Lebanon," *Military Review*, Vol. 87, No. 5.

70. Hassan M. Fattah, "Arab League Criticizes Hezbollah for Attacks," *The New York Times*, 2006, available from *www.nytimes.com/2006/07/17/world/africa/17iht-arabs.2224812.html?_r=0*.

71. Nasrallah, "We wouldn't have snatched soldiers if we thought it would spark war," *Haaretz*, available from *www.haaretz.com/news/nasrallah-we-wouldn-t-have-snatched-soldiers-if-we-thought-it-would-spark-war-1.199556*.

72. Sayyed Hassan Nasrallah speech at the Divine Victory Rally held in Beirut, Lebanon, available from *english.alahednews.com.lb/essaydetailsf.php?eid=709&fid=11*.

73. Hezbollah has built its own network of communication parallel to the state's one; it wanted full secrecy and maximum operational security for its war against Israel, available from *arabic.people.com.cn/31662/6405199.html*.

74. According to Max Weber, one of the major features of the state is to monopolize the coercive force within a delimited recognized and legitimate territory.

75. Nasrallah May 7th speech.

76. Therese Sfeir, "Nasrallah Hails May 7 as 'Glorious Day' for Resistance," *Daily Star*, available from *www.dailystar.com.lb/News/Politics/May/16/Nasrallah-hails-May-7-as-glorious-day-for-Resistance.ashx#axzz2e8Bq6u4h*.

77. Letter dated May 22, 2008, from the Permanent Observer of the League of Arab States to the United Nations addressed to the President of the Security Council, available from *www.securitycouncilreport.org/atf/cf/%7B65BFCF9B-6D27-4E9C-8CD3-CF6E4FF96FF9%7D/Lebanon%20S2008392.pdf*.

78. I suggest reading James Barr, *A Line in the Sand: The Anglo-French Struggle for the Middle East, 1914-1948*, 1st Ed., New York: W. W. Norton & Company.

79. Sun Tzu, *The Art of War*, Book 3, "Attack By Stratagem," available from *suntzusaid.com/book/3*.

80. Nasrallah speech.

81. The Jihadists Sunnis consider the Shia as deviants from Islam, they are Infidels just as are the Christians.

82. Matthew Levitt and Aaron Y. Zelin, "Hizb Allah's Gambit in Syria," West Point, NY: U.S. Military Academy, August 27, 2013, available from *www.ctc.usma.edu/posts/hizb-allahs-gambit-in-syria.*

CHAPTER 6

THE CASE OF THE ISRAELIS AND PALESTINIANS

Eyal Pascovich

THE PALESTINIANS

It was Abba Eban, Israel's legendary Foreign Minister, who coined the famous quote "The Palestinian Arabs have never missed a chance of losing an opportunity [for peace]."[1] It seems that his observation keeps being true, even in the years that passed, during which the Palestinians have continued too long in vain for the realization of their nationality within the framework of an independent state.

There are many factors at the base of the Palestinians' failure thus far in achieving full realization of their national rights. The Palestinian leadership throughout the 20th century and in the beginning of the 21st—its nature, weaknesses, and the decisions it made over the years—played a considerable part in shaping the current reality. This particularly refers to Yasser Arafat, who led the National Palestinian Movement for 4 decades, from the 1960s until the beginning of the millennium; however, it also refers to the leaders who preceded Arafat and those who succeeded him.

Pre-Arafat Era.

The establishment of the State of Israel in 1948, its triumph in the Israeli War of Independence, and the Palestinian catastrophe that followed—the Nakba—

141

constitute a key traumatic event in the history of the Palestinian people. In the struggle between the two national movements — the Palestinian and the Jewish-Zionist — over the same piece of land, the triumphant movement was the one that had succeeded in establishing a leadership and institutional foundations for the budding state throughout nearly 3 decades of British Mandate.

In contrast, the National Palestinian Movement had suffered from a delayed national awakening,[2] an institutional weakness and a divided and conflicted leadership — largely between the two rivalry families, Husseini and Nashashibi, whose members held the most important positions in the Palestinian society during the British Mandate era. Among them emerged Haj Amin al-Husseini, who is considered the first Palestinian leader.

Haj Amin, member of the Jerusalemite al-Husseini family, was appointed Mufti of Jerusalem in the early-1920s, when he was only 26 years old, and later also President of the Supreme Muslim Council. These two roles positioned him as the highest religious authority — and to a large degree also the political one, though not without disagreements — for the Arabs of Palestine. During the 1920s, the Palestinians, under al-Husseini's leadership, steered clear from taking part in any representative institutions the British attempted to establish for the citizens of Palestine, both Jews and Arabs, although the Arabs' clear demographic advantage at the time would have granted them a nearly absolute dominance.

While violent events between Arabs and Jews in Palestine throughout most of the 1920s were not common, the 1929 Western Wall Uprising, which was incited, to a large degree by al-Husseini, had marked the beginning of the ongoing violence in the Israeli-Palestinian conflict. Al-Husseini had aspired—and succeeded—in utilizing these events to add a religious aspect to the national-territorial conflict in Palestine and by which to recruit the Arab countries and the Islamic world in favor of the Palestinians' struggle. The Western Wall Uprising strengthened al-Husseini's leadership although his rivals, mainly among the Nashashibi family, had continued to subvert him and consequently undermined the National Palestinian Movement's cohesiveness and strength.

Under al-Husseini's leadership, in 1936, the Palestinians initiated wide-ranging riots against both the Jewish residents and the British rule, an uprising that earned the title "The Great Arab Revolt."[3] Nevertheless, after 3 years of uprising, the Palestinians have lost more than they gained—they suffered many casualties, their economy was devastated, and even their minor political accomplishments rapidly dissipated. Historian Abd al-Wahab ak-Kayali lays the blame for the revolt's outcomes on the Palestinian leadership:

> The Palestinian nation's leadership did not rise to the level of challenges faced by it. It was characterized by narrow-mindedness, personal ambitiousness and submissiveness. It was unable to provide a true response to the fact that Britain had fully embraced the Zionist movement. . . . Rather, the political Palestinian leadership had nourished the division between clans and opposed recruiting the masses and organizing them in a revolutionary structure, a structure that may have been suitable for the confrontation with Zionism and colonialism.[4]

A devastating outcome of the 1936-39 revolt was the self-imposed or forced departure of most of the political Palestinian leaders from Palestine. Haj Amin al-Husseini was forced to leave as early as 1937 during a cessation in the revolt, in light of British attempts to arrest him. During World War II, he had established ties with Adolf Hitler and the German Nazi party, and his image gradually fell apart.[5] As al-Husseini's exile period became prolonged, his influence on the Palestinians' fate gradually declined until it finally came to an end. The Palestinians' tragedy is that their first national leader lived a long life and passed away in Lebanon in 1974, with the prime of his success far behind.[6]

Thus, during the most important years of the national struggle in Palestine, the years following World War II, the Palestinians were left orphaned. One of the leaders who remained in Palestine at the time, Jamal al-Husseini (also a member of the Husseini family), was one of the leading witnesses on their behalf in the hearings of the Anglo-American Committee of Inquiry on Palestine's affairs held in 1946. Al-Husseini's somewhat pale performance[7] and his choice of negative approach, attacking the Jewish community and furthermore strongly objecting to the British authorities, made a negative impression compared to the confident leadership of the two main witnesses on behalf of the Zionist movement, David Ben-Gurion and Chaim Weizmann, who later became the first Prime Minister and President of the State of Israel, respectively.

The unified and charismatic leadership of the Zionist movement in Palestine and its organized institutions, which comprised a fairly stable infrastructure for the budding Jewish state, had a meaningful effect on the outcome of the battle between the two nations over the Holy Land. The Anglo-American Committee hearings' failure was one of the factors that affected Britain in its decision to return the Mandate granted to it over Palestine to the United Nations (UN) General Assembly, which determined in November 29, 1947, on the British Mandate's end and the partition of Palestine into two independent states, Arab and Jewish. The latter was planned to span over 60 percent of Palestine's area, despite the fact that, at the time, the proportion of Jewish people did not exceed one-third of its population.

It was one of the greatest achievements of the Zionist diplomacy, and proof of the fiasco of the Palestinian leadership. The latter's weakness and lack of cohesiveness had gradually turned it into a marionette in the hands of the Arab states, and with their encouragement the Palestinians turned down the UN's Partition Plan.[8] Retrospectively, this tactic would prove to be devastating for generations to come; however, at that time, it may have been perceived as reasonable in light of the Arab states' pledge to take all necessary measures for the derailment of the Jewish State's establishment.

Immediately after the UN's approval of Palestine's partition plan, the first part of the 1948 war began. In this phase, the Palestinians fought alone, and the lack of strong leadership played against them.[9] After the establishment of the State of Israel in May 1948, the second part of the war began with the invasion of the Arabs' armies into Israel. Despite the Arabs' numerical superiority, Israel won the war, and the Palestinians experienced a catastrophe that earned the name Nakba (Arabic for disaster). Of the Palestinians, 730,000 became refugees in the Arab countries and about 160,000 remained in the Jewish State's territory and were absorbed into it as a minority.[10] The

Palestinian leadership vanished without a trace, and the Palestinian national struggle entered a long hibernation period.

The Palestinians would require a new leadership and a historical turning point in order to reawaken their national resurrection. Yasser Arafat and the 1967 Six-Day War intended to transpire this shift.

The Arafat Era.

Yasser Arafat (aka Abu Amar), the founding leader of the Palestinian people, was somewhat of an enigma. Indeed, countless books have been written about him, as well as quite a few biographies, however, many details about his life and personality remain in the dark.[11] Thus, for instance, Arafat insisted that he was born in Jerusalem, as would be appropriate for the Palestinians' leader. However, the common opinion is that he was actually born in Cairo, Egypt, in 1929 and spent only part of his childhood in Palestine. After completing his BA studies in civil engineering from an Egyptian university, he relocated to Kuwait in search for work. In Kuwait, he led a group of Palestinian students who, in the late-1950s, established the Fatah, reversed acronym of the Palestinian (National) Liberation Movement. In early-1965, the movement began executing low level acts of terror against Israel.

Concurrently with the Fatah's development as an independent organization, in 1964, the League of Arab States has established the Palestine Liberation Organization (PLO). The PLO was structured as a political organization right from the start. Ahmad Al-Shuqayri, who held several political positions during the British Mandate, was appointed PLO Chairman. Shuqayri's PLO leadership lasted only 3 years, during which he had attempted, unsuccessfully for the most part, to establish wide support among the Palestinian public and to develop fundamental military and civil contents. Shuqayri's image as one of PLO's founders has faded into obscurity by his successors, who portrayed him as a puppet-in-chief under the control of the Arab states.[12] Similarly, Yahya Hammuda, who served as Chairman after Shuqayri, did not leave his mark, and by the end of the 1960s, Arafat was elected PLO Chairman, and Fatah became the central organizational member in the PLO.

Now Arafat held two positions, PLO Chairman and Fatah Chairman. The combination of these two functions would play a significant role in Arafat's duality from 1974 onwards, when he will find himself, as PLO Chairman, as a legitimate political leader in the eyes of part of the international community, following the Arab League's and UN's recognition of the PLO as the sole representative of the Palestinian people.

However, as Fatah's Chairman, Arafat led the organization into a prolonged succession of terror attacks against Israel, particularly after the 1967 Six-Day War which resulted in Israel's takeover of the West Bank and Gaza Strip — from Jordan and Egypt, respectively — and the implementation of a military rule in these areas. The one million Palestinians in the occupied territories, most of whom were refugees from 1948 and their descendants, were united again under Israeli rule, and the Palestinian nationalism was reawakened. The occupation provided a booster for the use of terror; at this point, Fatah was joined by new terror organizations — the Palestinian Fronts — most of which have united under the PLO and Arafat's leadership.

Among the Fronts' leaders were a few of Arafat's arch enemies.[13] Nonetheless, Arafat had succeeded, thanks to his leadership skills and due to the shared desire for a Palestinian revolution, in uniting the different factions and in earning both internal and external legitimacy. Most Palestinian factions have accepted Arafat's authority, except for the Islamic faction which, at the time, was insignificant.[14] Arafat was successful in preventing the development of an alternative leadership by using "divide and conquer" tactics and by offering bribes, which resulted in the reinforcement of his political standing. In this way, Arafat firmly ruled the National Palestinian Movement almost until his last breath.

A review of Arafat's speeches throughout the 1970s, and even more so during the 1980s, reveals countless pragmatic expressions on the need for holding an international peace conference; the condemnation of violence; a call for Israel to join the negotiation table; and the recognition of the UN's resolutions on the Palestinian issue which, in fact, constitutes Arafat's recognition of the State of Israel in the pre-Six-Day War borders.[15] However, at the same time, Fatah and the Palestinian Fronts continued to execute terror attacks against Israel, mostly under Arafat's decree.

Despite its acquaintance with his shortcomings, the majority of the international community preferred to recognize Arafat's leadership. This was both for the lack of an alternative leader and thanks to his political and verbal maneuvers (Arafat was nicknamed "a political acrobat" and "the man with a thousand faces"), which enabled him to establish himself as a political leader, the only one among the Palestinians. In this essence, Ghassan al-Immam, a Saudi poet, has described him:

This old man is a player without a land or a playing field,
But he plays with all the balls and on all fields,
The catch is that in soccer he holds the ball in his hands,
He kicks the basketball with his feet,
He plays handball with his head,
When the referees call on him, he demands that someone else will take the rap,
He is never suspended because his game-plan is amusing,
He never sits on the bench because he is irreplaceable,
There's no one in the world that can foul like he does,
And when he loses the game, he wins the crowds' applause.[16]

Contrary to the international community's approach, Israel (and the United States) adhered to their refusal to recognize the PLO or to negotiate with it. Israel also refused to recognize the Palestinians' right for a state, and, at the most, offered them autonomy, as outlined in the 1978 Camp David Accords between Israel and Egypt (the Palestinians did not attend the Camp David summit). Israel encouraged the development of a moderate Palestinian leadership — municipal and political — in the Territories, though without much success. In any event, Israel preferred negotiating with Jordan on the Territories' future; however, the latter demanded to be handed back the entire West Bank and East Jerusalem.

Concurrently, a more nationalistic political leadership developed in the Territories, and another member of the famous al-Husseini family surfaced, Faisal Husseini. However, the latter's closeness to Arafat, in combination with the PLO's control over Palestinian politics from abroad,[17] prevented Husseini from being perceived as an alternative leader to Arafat, both by Israel and the Palestinians themselves.[18]

Despite the PLO and Arafat's leading role in the Palestinian national struggle, they were caught by surprise by the outbreak of the popular uprising in the Territories—the Intifada—in December 1987. To avoid the likelihood of the riots seeping into his territory as well, King Hussein of Jordan had announced a couple of months later, in July 1988, of his country's disengagement from the West Bank and Jerusalem, and that he was no longer a partner in the attempts to resolve the Palestinian problem. PLO now stood alone. Nonetheless, Israel remained steadfast in its refusal to negotiate directly with it; on the other hand, the United States recognized the PLO in November 1988, following an additional moderation in the views presented by the PLO and Arafat.[19]

Another accomplishment of Arafat was the 1991 assembly of an international conference on peace in the Middle East, the Madrid Conference, with the participation of Israel and the Arab states. Indeed, the PLO and Arafat, who had been calling for the assembly of such a conference for years, did not directly attend it because of Israel's objection; nevertheless, Arafat controlled every move made by the Palestinian delegates in the joint Jordanian-Palestinian delegation.

Indeed, the Madrid Conference and the subsequent bilateral talks did not produce any progress. Nevertheless, the two were essential for setting the stage for the initiation of the Oslo, Norway, process, which would make the realization of the Palestinian national dream closer than ever.

Arafat and the Oslo Process.

Israel's recognition of the PLO in 1993, the signing of the two Oslo accords between the two sides, and the establishment of the Palestinian Authority (PA), headed by Arafat—all constituted the greatest accomplishment of all times for Arafat, the PLO and the Palestinian people, in spite of the PLO and Arafat's crisis in the beginning of the 1990s following 1) their inability to control the Intifada; 2) the fall of the Soviet Union, which provided the PLO financial and diplomatic support; and 3) the Arab States' termination of financial support for the PLO (due to Arafat's support of Saddam Hussein during the first Gulf War). Relinquishing the use of terror and opting for diplomacy brought the PLO and Arafat back into the center stage.

At this point, Arafat was holding three roles: Fatah Chairman, PLO Chairman, and the Palestinian Authority (PA) Chairman (although he preferred the title President). As someone who dedicated his life for the Palestinian national struggle and did not see any disparity between his own interests and those of the Palestinian people,[20] Arafat carried on with his past behavior patterns in his new role, too. He maintained his old centralized work style, and continued bribing his internal opponents-competitors or belittling them by using "divide and conquer" tactics. Needless to say, he kept on treating the PA funds, which originated mainly from the European Union and the Arab states, as if they were his own (just as he had done before with PLO funds)—although his corruption was never personal but rather political; Arafat himself continued living in somewhat of asceticism.

151

The onset of the Oslo process brought about a great deal of antagonism from the political opposition in Israel and the PA.[21] The Islamic movements in the Territories—the Palestinian Islamic Jihad (PIJ) and the rising power, the Hamas movement, which was established with the Intifada outbreak at the end of 1987—did not follow the PLO and Arafat's lead and sought to prevent the danger, in their view, in relinquishing the dream of Greater Palestine. From 1994, the two organizations began executing suicide terror attacks in Israeli cities—an unknown weapon in the Palestinian arena at the time—which brought about a decline in the support for the peace process among the Israeli public. Arafat was accused of turning a blind eye and not being firm with Hamas and the PIJ, and that the two constitute for him—as someone who always waved two flags, diplomatic and terror—a type of alternative for the Fatah's violent activity against Israel (Fatah laid down its arms by force of the Oslo Accords).

On the other hand, it was claimed that Arafat had difficulty employing harsh measures against the Islamic movements out of fear that the latter would turn against him and put his rule at risk. When he felt that Hamas and PIJ went too far, for instance, in the wave of terror attacks on Israeli cities in February-March 1996, he definitely employed a firm hand against them. But then again, it was too late. Several months before, Israeli Prime Minister Yitzchak Rabin had been murdered by an Israeli assassin who was seeking to put an end to the peace process. Rabin's substitute in office, Shimon Peres, a member of the left wing Avoda party and one of Oslo's architects, had lost the May 1996 elections to the right wing Likud party candidate, Benjamin Netanyahu, who was opposed to the

Oslo process; this was a direct result of the Hamas and PIJ's terror attacks, and exactly what they set out to accomplish.

The opponents of the peace process on both sides have attained their objectives, and the Oslo process derailed during the second half of the 1990s. The original timetables were disrupted, and the trust between the two parties gradually shattered. Only the return of the Israeli Avoda party to government in May 1999 and the appointment of its leader, Ehud Barak, to Prime Minister breathed new life into the peace process.

In July 2000, U.S. President Bill Clinton assembled the two sides, headed by Barak and Arafat, to a peace summit in the presidential country retreat of Camp David. This summit's goal was to discuss, for the first time, the three core issues in the Israeli-Palestinian conflict — the borders, Jerusalem, and the Palestinian refugees — and to sign on a permanent peace agreement to end the conflict. The failure of the summit has brought about a renewal of the blood cycle between the two sides; the establishment of a Palestinian state, which seemed to be close at hand, has turned once again into a distant aspiration.

The Camp David Summit, the Outbreak of the Al-Aqsa Intifada, and the Twilights of the Arafat Era.

The narrative surrounding the events that led to the 2000 Camp David summit's failure and to the unprecedented round of violence that started 2 months later, which is known as the Al-Aqsa Intifada, is controversial. According to the Israeli account, Arafat was offered a generous agreement, including far-reaching Israeli concessions, territorial and others.

However, Arafat, as usual, avoided making a decision in favor of ending the conflict and instead opted to return to terror, perhaps out of hope that it would enable him to return later on to the negotiation table in a better position.[22]

Clinton had also placed the blame for the summit's failure on Arafat.[23] On the other hand, others describe the situation in a different way, perhaps slightly more balanced, and claim that the root of the failure lies in the somewhat-rushed way the summit was organized, lacking sufficient preparation and missing several essential intermediate stages. Arafat was dragged into the summit against his will, following Barak and specifically Clinton, who was determined to end his second term in the White House with a positive accord. Some also criticized the behavior of these two at the summit — Barak who thought, in his overconfidence, that he would be able to coerce his conditions for a peace agreement on the Palestinians[24] (who claimed, on their part, that Barak's offered agreement had not met their needs and expectations whatsoever[25]); and Clinton, whose subjective, pro-Israeli mediation barred, from the onset, any chance for reaching a Palestinian willingness to accept his ideas for compromise.

Indeed, Arafat's suspicion toward his Israeli counterpart and toward the American mediator played a significant role in the summit's failure. With all the weight of responsibility on his shoulders, Arafat chose to postpone the final decision. In the same vain, Akram Haniyeh, a member of the Palestinian Delegation to the summit, wrote:

On those sunny days, Arafat led one of the most difficult battles of his life. . . . He comprehended the enormous burden of the mandate that was handed to him as well as the extent of the deposit entrusted in his hands as a leader of a nation, whose strength and source of pride stem from the fact that it is protecting the holy sites existing on its land. [Arafat's] comprehension should not be interpreted as arrogance but rather as an understanding of the full weight of responsibility, because he entered this battle on behalf of the Palestinian people, the Arab states, the Islamic nation as well as the Christians. . . . He had to protect the holy city [Jerusalem, or al-Quds in Arabic], which was tied with important figures, from Caliph Umar ibn Al-Khattab to ala a-Din al-Ayyubi, and with his people he had to fight the battle alone.[26]

Additional narrative differences refer to the issue surrounding Arafat's involvement in the outbreak of the Al-Aqsa Intifada in September 2001. The narrative developed by Ehud Barak and adopted by the Israeli public and media, accuses Arafat of being responsible for the violent events' outbreak and escalation. The latter included violent clashes between Palestinian security forces and the Israeli military, and the return of suicide terror attacks into Israeli streets, this time not only by the Islamic organizations but for the first time also by the Fatah. Barak and Ariel Sharon from the Likud right wing party, who replaced him in office as Israeli Prime Minister after the elections held in February 2002, ascertained that Arafat was no longer a negotiation partner (the last attempt for negotiation between Barak and Arafat was the Taba Conference in January 2002, after the violent events' eruption, however, this negotiation never stood a chance in light of the upcoming elections in Israel).

Nevertheless, there is yet another narrative. High ranking officials in the Israeli military Intelligence Directorate, Aman, claimed that the violent events have erupted spontaneously — a day after a provocative visit of Ariel Sharon, then Head of the Israeli political opposition, in the Temple Mount — and not as a pre-planned plot by Arafat. Furthermore, they claim that Arafat had difficulties in controlling the violent events, and elements within the Palestinian security forces and the Fatah movement that inflamed the events did not follow Arafat's orders. However, this narrative did not fare well with Barak's agenda and later on with Sharon's, and Aman's leading echelon aligned with them and rewrote its intelligence assessments.[27]

The continuation of the violent events led Israel to take action against the PA's government institutions and security forces, and the PA's strength increasingly weakened. Under Israel's lead, a public diplomacy campaign was launched with the goal of undermining Arafat's image while accusing him of corruption and assisting terrorism.[28] Arafat spent his last years imprisoned, in essence, in the Mukataa' (the Palestinian governmental offices in Ramallah), condemned and isolated from the world and, in many aspects, also from his own people. Appropriately for the Yasser Arafat myth, the cause of his death in November 2004, at the age of 75, was also never entirely clarified — an unusual blood disease, AIDS, or perhaps another reason (the Palestinians claim that he was poisoned by Israel, adding a touch of martyrdom to his death).[29]

Examination of Arafat's image is not without risks. An examination of a myth or a symbol may be interpreted as a premeditated act: as an aspiration for delegitimacy, iconoclasm, or alternatively — as worship and reverence. The mere point of view may determine the outcome.

The most important aspect is the way in which the Palestinians themselves perceived Arafat and the mark he had left on them (and not how much he was loathed by Israel). Hence, in this case, the myth may be more important than reality, since Arafat's main role was to make an impression, to become a symbol that translates the Palestinians' dreams and desires into a historical reality.[30]

All of the following, and more, contributed to the creation of the myth of Yasser Arafat.

1. Arafat's dismissal of his personal identity in favor of the Palestinian revolution and the mystery surrounding his personal life as well as his intents and final goals of the Palestinian national struggle (which possibly were not completely clear to him either);

2. His intentional ungroomed appearance and his insistence on wearing a keffiyeh and military uniforms, even after he was recognized as a political leader; and,

3. The countless times he survived elimination attempts by his opponents from within and without (including by Israel, evidence for the importance it conferred on him and on his leadership).[31]

The duality in his words and actions throughout the years, even after the onset of diplomatic dialogue between him and Israel, had served well both his supporters and opponents. He provided bountiful justifications for the claims made by both sides. Ironically, Arafat was concurrently referred to as both the problem and the solution; one could not live with or without him. The leadership void he left behind him is confirmation of these observations.

Finally, in the eyes of the Palestinians, despite the fact that it may seem as if Arafat's image was slightly tarnished during his last years, he would be remembered as the greatest Palestinian leader of all times; as the one who led his people for more than 40 stormy years, filled with impressive accomplishments and magnificent failures, almost within a hand's reach of a realization of their aspiration for national independence.

Post-Arafat Era.

Arafat did not nurture a natural successor during his lifetime — not among PLO's veteran generation nor among the younger generation in Fatah. His position as PLO Chairman was filled by Mahmoud Abbas (aka Abu Mazan), a veteran member of the organization. In January 2005, Abbas won the majority of votes in the elections for PA Chairman.

Unlike his predecessor, Abbas benefits from an image of a pragmatic, moderate, and honest man, and therefore he receives the international community's trust. However, Abbas is lacking the prestige, respect, and reverence Arafat received from the Palestinian people, and it is doubtful whether he would be able to lead a diplomatic step of historical compromise with Israel which will force the Palestinian side to also make painful concessions — of the Greater Palestine dream and the realization of the 1948 Palestinian refugees' right of return. Abbas, indeed, received acrid responses from the Arab world and the Palestinian arena on a specific quote he had made in November 2012 in a TV interview that was interpreted as if he recognized the fact that the right of return would not be realized. However, these responses quickly faded away — evidence, perhaps, for the fact that everyone understands that Abbas lacks the public mandate to make a decision on this issue.[32]

Abbas' weakness allowed Hamas to raise its head and to confront the Fatah and the PA's security apparatuses, an act it did not dare do when Arafat—who benefited from the Hamas' reverence—was alive. Initially, this Islamic movement won the elections held in January 2006 for the Palestinian Legislative Council, which is the Palestinian Parliament. One of Hamas' top officials, Ismail Haniyah, was appointed the Palestinian Prime Minister, the second most important position in the PA (this position was tailored at the request of Israel in 2003, when Arafat was still alive, with the intent to bypass him[33]). In light of the PLO, Fatah and the PA Institutions' weakness—among other things, due to Israeli activity against them during the Al-Aqsa Intifada years—Hamas successfully carried out a revolt in the Gaza Strip in June 2007; it removed Fatah from government and instituted an independent government under the leadership of Ismail Haniyah, a government which was never recognized by Israel. In essence, the PA was divided in two, and in fact, Abbas is now governing the West Bank territories only.

Hamas' victory in the elections and gaining control over Gaza brought about pragmatization in the movement's viewpoints. Its leaders, headed by Haniyah and Khaled Mashal (head of Hamas' Political Bureau and, in the past, a target of a failed Israeli assassination attempt[34]), have started to exhibit pragmatic standpoints, at least outwardly,[35] and the scope of terror against Israel considerably declined. However, Israel stood firm in its refusal to have contacts with Hamas, and stood by the increasingly weakening Abbas as the sole negotiation partner.

Unlike Arafat, Abbas had placed all his hopes on diplomacy while vigorously opposing terror and vio-

lence (during his time in office, the Al-Aqsa Intifada —
which did not produce any accomplishments for the
Palestinians — came to an end). Nevertheless, he was
faced with an Israeli leadership suffering from great
flaws too. Indeed, during Ehud Olmert's term in office
as Israeli Prime Minister (2006-09), negotiations with
the PA (which, as previously mentioned, since 2007
had control over the West Bank only) was renewed,
and a great deal of progress was actually made in talks
between the two sides on the core issues, including —
perhaps — far-reaching Israeli concessions.[36] However,
like Abbas, Olmert, too, earned very little public support due to his part in Israel's failure in the 2006 Lebanon War and his alleged involvement in several corruption affairs, which eventually forced him to resign
from office. His old-new successor as Prime Minister,
Benjamin Netanyahu, declared his intentions to promote the idea of "two states for two nations,"[37] however, in fact, he did nearly nothing to fulfill it.

With no other options, Abbas was forced to bypass
Israel and turn to international channels. In 2011, the
PA submitted a request to the UN Security Council to
approve its acceptance as a full UN member independent state on the basis of the 1967 borders (hence —
pre-Six-Day War).[38] Nevertheless, this tactic, too, produced limited accomplishments only.[39]

Abbas suffered an additional blow in April 2013
with the resignation of his right-hand man in recent
years, Palestinian Prime Minister Salam Fayyad.
Fayyad, who received a great deal of trust from the
international community, the United States, and Israel, was appointed in 2001 during the Arafat era as Finance Minister in the PA government. He had the job
of cleaning up corruption and establishing appropriate administrative procedures (in the past he served

160

as the International Monitory Fund's representative in the Territories). Concurrently with his successful term in office as Finance Minister, Fayyad was appointed the PA's Prime Minister (PM) in the summer of 2007, following Hamas' takeover of Gaza and Ismail Haniyah's appointment as PM in the Hamas government in Gaza. Fayyad, who was perceived as a U.S. ally and of the West, never gained popularity among the Palestinians or among the governing political party in the West Bank, the Fatah, in which he has never been a member. However, during his term in office as PM, he was very successful in developing the Palestinian economy and building the governmental institutions for the budding state — two areas that were neglected during Arafat's era.[40] Fayyad's resignation has left Abbas alone, once again.

Thus, the Palestinian people continue to shift, decade after decade, from cautious optimism to pessimism and despair which are so familiar to them — despair from Israel, that keeps on piling obstacles for peace; despair from the Arab states and the international community that deserted the Palestinians; and despair from their own leadership, that has failed, so far, in realizing their national dream.

It seems that both Palestinians and Israelis aspire to a different leadership on both sides — strong, far-sighted, ready to make painful historical compromises and having a wide-ranging internal legitimacy — a leadership that would end the long lasting conflict between these two nations.

ENDNOTES - CHAPTER 6

1. Abba Eban, "International Affairs in the Modern Age," *The New Diplomacy*, Winter 1983-84, p. 229.

2. One of the leading researchers of Palestinian history in our time, Professor Rashid Khalidi from Colombia University, disagrees with the consensus among Israeli historians, according to which, the Palestinian nationality awakened mainly as a reaction to the Zionist thriving. Rashid Khalidi, *Palestinian Identity: The Construction of Modern National Consciousness*, New York: Columbia University Press, 1997.

3. To intensify this uprising's popular and national nature, it is often referred to in Palestinian literature as "The Great Palestinian Revolt." Israeli historiography refers to this revolt as "the bloody clashes" — to diminish its significance.

4. Abd al-Wahab ak-Kayali, *Ta'rikh Falastin al-Khdith* (*The History of Modern Palestine*), in Arabic, Beirut, Lebanon, 1985, p. 313.

5. See Klaus Gensicke, Alexander Fraser Gunn, trans., *The Mufti of Jerusalem and the Nazis: The Berlin Years*, London, UK: Vallentine Mitchell, 2011.

6. For a more detailed account of Haj Amin al-Hussaini life and ideology, see, for instance, Zvi Elpeleg, David Harvey, trans., *The Grand Mufti: Haj Amin al-Hussaini, Founder of the Palestinian National Movement*, London, UK: Frank Cass, 1993.

7. Jamal al-Hussaini had also decided to emphasize Haj Amin al-Hussaini's absence:

> The Arabs [in Palestine] assume that in your hearings, you wanted to hear the Arabs' opinion from their well-known leaders and representatives. However, in this inquiry they perceive themselves lacking the presence of their first and foremost leader, the Grand Mufti, who is irreplaceable. . . .

See Esriel Carlebach, ed., Anglo-American Committee of Inquiry on Jewish Problems in Palestine and Europe [in Hebrew], Vol. 2, Tel Aviv, Israel: Leinman, 1946, p. 352.

8. Jamal al-Hussaini has declared in this context that "the partition line shall be nothing but line of fire and blood." See Rony E. Gabbay, *A Political Study of the Arab-Jewish Conflict: The Arab*

Refugee Problem (A Case Study), Geneva, Switzerland, and Paris, France: E. Droz, 1959, p. 58.

9. Thus, Albert Hourani, the notable expert on Middle Eastern Affairs, wrote, based on the writings of Musa al-Alami, one of the most respected Arabs in Palestine:

> The Palestinian Arabs failed, because they have fought peasants and guerilla war with outdated methods, whereas their opponents fought a totally modern war. They lacked central command, as well as unification around the goal, they had limited weapons, they were untrained and had nearly no experienced officers. There was no unified action, each city or village defended itself; not one of them had sent assistance to the other; and the districts far from the battlefront remained inactive, while others were conquered one by one.

See Albert Hourani, "Arab Refugees and the Future of Israel," BBC, as brought by *Haaretz* daily newspaper (in Hebrew), December 1, 1949.

10. A lively debate exists among historians surrounding the number of Palestinian refugees and particularly surrounding the causes for their exodus. Researchers identified with the "New Historians" group, whose studies have been published in the last 2 decades, point out to a series of deportation acts of Palestinians executed by Israel during the 1948 war. See in this reference Benny Morris' monumental book, *The Birth of the Palestinian Refugee Problem Revisited*, 2nd Ed., Cambridge, UK: Cambridge University Press, 2004. Avi Shlaim, another "New Historian," claims that the results of the war were predetermined by a conspiracy concocted by Israel and Jordan, both of which wished to prevent the establishment of a Palestinian entity. See Avi Shlaim, *Collusion across the Jordan: King Abdullah, the Zionist Movement, and the Partition of Palestine*, New York: Columbia University Press, 1988. The "New Historians" stirred up fierce opposition among some of the researchers studying this era; See, for instance, Efraim Karsh, *Fabricating Israeli History: The 'New Historians'*," London, UK: F. Cass 1997.

11. See in this context, Arafat's 1983 interview with Arab journalists:

> Who exactly are you?
> I am a fighter in the ranks of the Palestinian
> revolution.
> Is your name Yasser Arafat?
> That is the name by which I have been known since my
> university days.
> Where are you from?
> From the very heart of the Palestinian people.
> The Palestinians would like to know more about their
> leader; permit us to ask once again who are you?
> I am a son of the Palestinian people and a fighter in the
> ranks of the revolution.

See Danny Rubinstein, Dan Leon, trans., *The Mystery of Arafat*, South Royalton, VT: Steerforth Press, 1995, p. 25.

12. For this reason precisely, only a few works have been written about Shuqayri. See, for instance: Yaniv Ronen, *The Forgotten Leader: A Biography of Ahmad Al-Shuqayri* [in Hebrew], a Ph.D. Thesis, Bar-Ilan University, Ramat-Gan, Israel, 2010.

13. I.e., George Habash, a Christian, who led the Popular Front for the Liberation of Palestine. Among the Fronts' leaders and members were many Christians, all of whom followed Arafat's leadership, who was Muslim.

14. For this reason, the Palestinian National Movement and its different components — PLO, Fatah, and the Fronts — earned the title "the secular faction."

15. I.e., in his first speech before the UN General Assembly in 1974, Arafat said:

> We do not wish one drop of either Arab or Jewish blood to
> be shed; neither do we delight in the continuation of killing,
> which would end once a just peace, based on our people's
> rights, hopes and aspirations had been finally established.
> . . . I appeal to you to enable our people to establish national
> independent sovereignty over its own land. Today I have

come bearing an olive branch and a freedom-fighter's gun.
Do not let the olive branch fall from my hand. . . . War flares
up in Palestine, and yet it is in Palestine that peace will be
born.

See *unispal.un.org/UNISPAL.NSF/0/A238EC7A3E13EED18525624
A007687EC*. In his second speech before the UN General Assembly in 1988, he said:

Our National Council stressed the need to convene an international conference on the Middle East problem, with the
issue of Palestine as its core . . . the international conference
will convene in accordance with Security Council Resolutions 242 and 338 and on the basis of guaranteeing the legitimate national and political rights of the Palestinian people,
the foremost being their right to self-determination. . . . The
Palestinian National Council reiterated its rejections of terrorism; it reiterated its rejection of terrorism of all kinds,
including state terrorism. . . . In my capacity as Chairman of
the PLO, I declare from here once more: I condemn terrorism in all its forms. . . .

Available from *www.al-bab.com/arab/docs/pal/pal5.htm*.

16. Rubinstein, p. 35.

17. Until 1982, the PLO was located in Lebanon. Following
the Israeli invasion to Lebanon in that year, it relocated to Tunisia.

18. More on local politics in the Territories from 1967 until
the end of the 1980s can be found in Emile Sahliyeh, *In Search
of Leadership: West Bank Politics Since 1967*, Washington, DC: The
Brookings Institution, 1988.

19. In a symbolic act following King Hussein's speech on Jordan's disengagement from the West Bank, the Palestinian National Council declared in November 15, 1988, on the establishment
of the State of Palestinian. The declaration of independence reads:

The State of Palestine herewith declares that it believes in the
settlement of regional and international disputes by peaceful means. . . . It rejects the threat or use of force, violence
and terrorism against its territorial integrity or political in-

dependence, as it also rejects their use against the territorial integrity of other states. . . .

Available from *www.al-bab.com/arab/docs/pal/pal3.htm*.

20. Thus, for instance, Arafat explained the fact that he remained unmarried until his 60s by saying that he is married to a beautiful woman named Palestine, or alternatively — that all Palestinian women are his wives and all the children of Palestine are his own. His marriage in 1990 to Suha Tawil, a Christian woman 34 years his junior, was originally kept a secret. The Palestinian public and leadership never received Suha as their own, and rumors surrounded the nature of their relationship. The two have one daughter named Zahwa.

21. Israeli political opposition claimed that Arafat's support of the Oslo process and his recognition of Israel were nothing but a conspiracy as part of the "stages theory," which means — in their view — that Arafat's consent to the two states' solution was a tactic and temporary one and an intermediate stage toward the final stage: realization of the dream of Greater Palestine and the annihilation of the State of Israel.

22. Shlomo Ben Ami, Israeli Delegation member to the Camp David summit, later wrote the following: "The Palestinian side is unable, as long as it is led by Arafat, to make a historical decision to end the conflict." See Shlomo Ben Ami *A Front Without a Rearguard: A Voyage to the Boundaries of the Peace Process* (in Hebrew), Tel Aviv, Israel: Miskal-Yedioth Ahronoth Books and Chemed Books, 2004, p. 534.

23. Bill Clinton, *My Life*, New York: Alfred A. Knopf, 2004, pp. 915-916, 937-938, 944-945.

24. See, for instance, the analysis of Ron Pundak, one of the Oslo Accord's architects:

Barak is a man with amazing powers of concentration and analysis, used to coping with novel and stressful situations. He may have failed precisely because of these qualities. His approach to negotiation had elements of arrogance and the fallacy that he alone understood the 'big picture'. His strategic vision and historical insight failed him as he attempted to impose his operating style on partners who were not ready for it.

See Ron Pundak, "From Oslo to Taba: What Went Wrong?" *Survival*, Vol. 43, No. 3, Autumn 2001, p. 40.

25. Dennis Ross, *The Missing Peace: The Inside Story of the Fight for Middle East Peace*, New York: Farrar, Straus and Giroux, 2004, p. XII.

26. Ben Ami, pp. 236-237.

27. Ephraim Lavie, "Intelligence Activity in the Palestinian Arena — A Critical Assessment" (in Hebrew), *Mabat Malam*, a journal for intelligence and security affairs of the Israel Heritage & Commemoration Center (IICC), No. 52, December 2008, p. 31-32.

28. This public diplomacy campaign was led by an entity tied to the Israeli military Intelligence Directorate — the Intelligence and Terrorism Information Center, available from *www.terrorism-info.org.il/en/index.aspx*. This led to criticism according to which the Intelligence should not be dealing with public diplomacy.

29. Arafat was buried in Ramallah after a funeral ceremony in Cairo. The Palestinians' request to bury him in Jerusalem was denied by Israel. The funeral was characterized by disorder and uncontrolled outburst of emotions from the Palestinian crowd.

30. Rubinstein, pp. xii-xiii.

31. In addition, Arafat also survived a plane crash in the Libyan Desert in April 1992; appropriately, Arafat was nicknamed "the man with nine lives."

32. Harriet Sherwood, "Mahmoud Abbas Outrages Palestinian Refugees by Waiving His Right to Return," *The Guardian*, November 4, 2012, available from *www.theguardian.com/world/2012/nov/04/mahmoud-abbas-palestinian-territories*.

33. Initially Mahmoud Abbas held this position, and after a few months he was replaced by Ahmed Qurei (aka Abu Alaa), also a member of PLO's veteran echelon. Qurei held this position until the 2006 Legislative Council elections.

34. Many of Hamas' military and political leaders, among them the movement's founder, Ahmed Yassin, were assassinated by Israel during the 1990s and particularly during the Al-Aqsa Intifada in the beginning of the 2000s.

35. See for example, Amira Hass, "Haniyeh: Hamas willing to accept Palestinian state with 1967 borders," *Haaretz*, November 9, 2008, available from *www.haaretz.com/news/haniyeh-hamas-willing-to-accept-palestinian-state-with-1967-borders-1.256915.*

36. Condoleezza Rice, *No Higher Honor: A Memoir of my Years in Washington*, New York: Broadway Paperbacks, 2011, pp. 650-656. Later on, Olmert claimed that the two sides were very close to signing a final peace agreement, however, Abbas' hesitance thwarted it. See Avi Issacharoff, "The Hope, the Fear and the Accusations: The Peace Agreement that Remained on the Napkin," *Walla*, May 24, 2013, available from *news.walla.co.il/?w=//2644736.*

37. See, for example, Netanyahu's address in Bar-Ilan University, June 14, 2009, available from *mfa.gov.il/MFA/PressRoom/2009/Pages/Address_PM_Netanyahu_Bar-Ilan_University_14-Jun-2009.aspx.*

38. See the transcript of Abbas' speech before the UN General Assembly, available from *www.un.int/wcm/content/site/palestine/cache/offonce/pid/28905.*

39. In October 2011, Palestine was accepted as a full member of the United Nations Educational, Scientific and Cultural Organization. In November 2012, the PA's status in the UN was upgraded from a nonstate observer entity to a nonmember observer state, available from *www.unesco.org/new/en/media-services/single-view/news/general_conference_admits_palestine_as_unesco_member_state/#.Uh2d6NxBRdg;* and *www.un.org/ga/search/view_doc.asp?symbol=A/RES/67/19.*

40. See Salam Fayyad, "Why I'm Building Palestine," *Foreign Policy*, Vol. 183, December 2010, p. 60.

PART III:

CONCLUSIONS AND RECOMMENDATIONS

CHAPTER 7

CONCLUSION AND RECOMMENDATIONS

Anastasia Filippidou

Leadership is essentially a human-centered activity comprising a number of elements — leaders, followers, context — all with different personalities and attributes. One of the main arguments of this book is that the most important factors that distinguish effective leaders often lay largely outside the control of an individual leader (context, resources, circumstances, etc.). Although a leader must have the ability to exploit the opportunities offered by external factors, a leader, irrespective of how good, cannot always really guarantee effectiveness by his own actions. Leadership perceptions help form decisionmakers' views, but they also prescribe political attitudes and behaviors. States may fail to cooperate even if they have compatible aims and preferences, because decisionmakers make incorrect inferences about their motives and intentions.[1]

THE PRAGMATISM OF AN ETHICAL FOREIGN POLICY

Main questions that arise from the research are: Is the foreign policy of the United States toward the Middle East achieving its objectives? If not, does fault lie with the theory or the execution? U.S. foreign policy toward the Middle East seems to have two images: one is what Christopher Lasch[2] called in the 1970s "the culture of narcissism" and the other is a feeling of insecurity expressed as elevating threats into existential ones. Both images have led to unsuitable and wrong policies. The United States has alternated a foreign policy in the Middle East of cooperation and confrontation and has been consistent at playing the "divide and rule" game contributing to existing divisions or creating new ones. As a result, often seemingly rational foreign policy decisions have failed to deliver the expected outcomes. Partiality and unfairness can hurt both the realist part of the U.S. foreign policy agenda by diminishing its actual power as well as the idealist portion of it and by undermining the U.S. appeal as the embodiment of certain ideas and values.

Historically U.S. foreign policy has identified the lack of democracy as a central cause of the problems in the Middle East. However, the uncompromising stance of imposing the right type of democracy has been and remains unlikely to succeed in the Middle East. This has led to accusations of double standards and as J. Mann points out "most of the other governments in the region, including US's long-time partners in Saudi Arabia and Egypt, could not meet the democratic standard Bush was setting for the Palestinians."[3] According to K. Dalacoura, "democracy promotion policies have limited outcomes because neither a politically neutral nor a more forceful approach can initiate reform if it is not already under way for domestic reasons."[4] After all, a political system is only one of the many facets of a functioning state, and actually it is often a subservient facet in an Islamic state. As Colin Gray argues, "there is no prospect that major potential belligerents will grow rapidly into the character of liberal democracies."[5]

At times U.S. foreign policy has failed to recognize and accept the region's cultural diversity, the power of outward and inward focused Islam, and its traditions which differ fundamentally from the West. Policy planning and implementation seem to have been quite uninformed by an understanding of the region's history, culture, and politics. Consequently, U.S. foreign policy in the Middle East has been misguided in its belief in a Western-style democratization, and it has suffered from being simplistic and idealistic in its approach to extremely complex realities. Difficulties arise if the terms Islam and democracy are used in a monolithic manner rather than acknowledging the flexibility and adaptability and "the diversity of actual experience."[6] Homogeneity is neither possible, nor should it be desirable. Past attempts to introduce different types of governance such as socialism and nationalism have each met with differing degrees of enthusiasm within the Middle East. However, common to all was the deep impact of Islam. This is also true for democracy which cannot hope to retain its Western secular ideals as it is absorbed and adapted by Muslim societies.

Monocausal explanations for foreign policy provide simplistic analyses and misleading decisions. There appear to be a number of paradoxes U.S. foreign policy has to deal with. The first paradox is that, although the United States needs an ally in a strategically vital region such as the Middle East, the region is hostile also because of such an alliance, which often leads to accusations of U.S. double standards. However, the second paradox is that despite the low standing of the United States among many in the Middle East, only a U.S. President appears to have the authority, legitimacy, and power to bring conflicting sides together for meaningful talks. The third paradox is when the United States adopts a more insular foreign policy, there are calls for the "responsibility" of the powerful "to do something"; however, if the United

States interferes, it is accused of meddling and of partiality.

Following from this, the fourth paradox is for the United States to try and maintain the status quo, but at the same time not being able to affect the change necessary to achieve this goal. The problem is that the very status of the United States denotes the existence of a distinct imbalance of power and the need to maintain this imbalance in order to prolong this status. As Eagleton puts it, "the task of political hegemony is to produce the very forms of subjecthood which will form the basis of political unity."[7] This nonetheless has led to charges of neo-imperialism. The fifth paradox that has caused controversy, objection, and accusation of double standards is the application of military power in order to promote and establish democratic regimes in strategic areas, according to the United States.

The sixth paradox for U.S. foreign policy decision-maker is to try and help a Middle Eastern country, on this occasion, however without meddling; that is to participate in a transition to peaceful politics but to have a selfless foreign policy and not try to influence domestic politics of the host country. The concluding paradox is the kind of leadership U.S. foreign policy-makers would prefer a host country to have. In the sense that if U.S. foreign policymakers were facing a strong leadership in a Middle Eastern country, although this strong leadership could on the one hand be less compromising, it could affect more effectively its own people and state and it could also influence more and shape the reactions of other people and states. If, on the other, U.S. policymakers were facing a weak leadership.

Although this weak leadership would be more malleable and possibly more prone to reach an agreement in a peace process, it could not really affect the actions of its own people; it would not be able, for instance, to maintain support and implement an agreement. Consequently, often U.S. foreign policymakers chose to support "reliable" leaders, which, in its turn, led to the promotion of preferred political systems. For instance, during the Cold War U.S. foreign policy supported "friendly" but authoritarian regimes as this was considered preferable to risking the emergence of an alternative regime, including a participatory regime, that would, however, have less friendly relations with the United States.[8] For instance, during the uprisings in Egypt in 2011, the looming question for U.S. foreign policymakers was whether to support Hosni Mubarak, the friendly authoritarian leader who represented an "island of stability" or to support the protesters seeking his ouster and thereby risking an unfriendly leader coming to power.[9]

More relevant to this point, and to the case studies of this research, is when U.S. foreign policymakers faced a similar dilemma following the victory of Hamas in the 2006 Palestinian elections, during which Washington overtly backed Mahmoud Abbas. This dilemma raised the question about the U.S. willingness to support outcomes of democratic elections given its outspoken rhetoric on the subject.[10] This links with the first paradox mentioned earlier and the accusations of double standards, rendering U.S. foreign policy efforts counterproductive. Hence, often the dilemma has been what kind of leadership to facilitate and support in a transitional phase: a strong or a weak one. However, since this decision will be contextual, a state must have a clear and "confident" foreign policy and must know what its own foreign policy vision and aim is. To this end, U.S. decisionmakers would have to decide if the driver behind their foreign policy is complacency or meaning. The former focuses on the present only, while the latter cares about the past and future actions and decisions. After all, as Joseph Nye observes, "having the resources of power does not guarantee that you will always get the outcome you want. To do so requires well designed strategies and skillful leadership"; in effect what Nye calls "smart power."[11]

U.S. foreign policymakers would have to constantly try and strike a balance and a harmony on the previously mentioned paradoxes, which is not always possible, even if there is will. In other words, U.S. foreign policy toward the Middle East will have to be adaptive and flexible on the one hand in order to show ability and will; but foreign policy will also have to be consistent on the other, so that it can show commitment and impartiality. For this to happen, however, and for foreign policy to be effective, it has to transcend party politics, and it has to bridge gaps between continuity and adaptability. Establishing and maintaining a "benevolent hegemony"[12] is not that easy.

Ideally, cooperation should be based on nonhegemonic attitudes and on the principle of reciprocity. Foreign policy, by its nature, involves a distorted, subjective image of reality inasmuch as it is formed based on national interests. For instance, perceptions toward Middle Eastern leaders have been highly subjective and varied within U.S. foreign policymakers. The same leader has been viewed and treated over time very differently by U.S. policymakers and advisors, even if the actions and behavior of the specific leader has remained consistent. Depending on who is governing or advising the United States, different leaders in the Middle East have been viewed as pariahs to be toppled or as pariahs to be tolerated or even promoted. Alternatively, pariahs with whom "we could do business with" one day are abandoned the next if perceptions of their utility changes. It is worth mentioning at this point that, historically, certain U.S. Presidents and decisionmakers appear to have developed what could be described as an obsessive behavior toward foreign leaders unrelated to the views of the current political establishment. Examples of this would include Fidel Castro, Saddam Hussein, and the Shah of Iran.

In an interdependent world where co-existence is vital, any state's foreign policy is constraint to one degree or another by a complex combination of external and domestic factors. Political domestic pressures inherent within a liberal democracy demand rapid results which, in turn, increase the likelihood of counterproductive and short-term tactics and approaches. Based on the above, an effective U.S. foreign policy would have to be reactive and proactive, depending on the context, situation, and circumstances.

The capacity of U.S. foreign policy to influence the behavior of a Middle East country (recipient country) depends on the interaction of the values the United States and the recipient attribute to an issue in which the United States attempts to exert influence. If an issue is of high value for the United States but low for the recipient and vice versa, there will be lack of trust, and thus the efforts of U.S. policymakers to influence the recipient country or efforts to establish cooperation between two countries are likely to fail. In this sense, there has to be an alignment of values between U.S. foreign policy aims and the recipient country's aims. Understandably, this would rarely be realistic, hence the suggestion is not to expect to have the same values as such, but for there to be empathy and acceptance of what is important for a recipient country and take that into consideration when forming foreign policy. This is not to be idealistic but just pragmatic, owing to interdependence and the need for coexistence.

The aim should be to achieve an altruistic, but at the same time pragmatic, foreign policy, and it is human capacity for justice that makes this possible. But, it is also human tendency toward injustice that makes it necessary. This would require constant knowledge, adaptation, flexibility, and a vision that transcends party politics and short-term policies. Given the complex environment within which decisionmakers operate, they rarely have the time to become proficient in the intricacies of foreign affairs. Thus for expediency, they tend to fall back to known constructs and to "how things are done here," with which they are familiar. Although this has been helpful at times, on many occasions old attitudes applied to new complex realities has been ineffective and inefficient. To promote its national interests in the long term, the United States might have to prioritize the local interests and almost altruistically help the regions overcome their internal divisions and problems. Why? Because of interdependence and the role history has attributed to the United States.

Main leadership theories have been reviewed in order to set the foundations for analysis of asymmetric leadership in transitional processes. The complicated and contradictory nature of asymmetric leadership in transitional processes is also emphasized. Different leadership types are examined, which has highlighted that, with the exception possibly of toxic leadership, it is difficult, if not impossible, to determine that a specific type is better than another in every situation. As such, it is apparent that some leadership styles are likely to be more effective in certain situations, and that a really effective leader is one who is able to determine the context of the situation and use the most effective leadership behavior required at the time. Effective leaders understand the context of the situation, add this to their understanding of themselves and others and adopt the appropriate skills and methods to achieve the desired outcome. Furthermore, categorizing a leader as one type or another runs the risk of being refuted as a result of shift in leadership behaviors dictated by broader political circumstances.

The concept of asymmetric leadership is based on the notion that, when political leaders find themselves in a position which compromises their intents, which is often the case during transition, they adapt and adjust to the new realities not necessarily because they accept the causes for change but because they need and want to survive. Leaders in transitional processes can find themselves in situations that compromise their intentions, which is often dictated by broader political circumstances and changes in the political environment. This idea of a constantly changing environment and its consequences validate the concept of asymmetric leadership. Asymmetric leadership can change its position in response to new issues coming to light during a peace process as well as in response to the needs and wants of themselves, their followers, and of their political adversaries.

A significant challenge for asymmetric leadership is the apparent failure of these leaders to adjust to normalization politics. This can be due to the unequal dynamic involved in asymmetric leadership, and the weaker position in which this type of leadership can find itself. When a transition process moves toward the normalization phase and the need for substantial reform decreases, leaders must adjust, and instead of leading, they have to become followers of the new structures, policies, and institutions. Insecurity in office and security out of office can make staying in peace a preferable option for political careers and lives. However as Chapters 3 and 4 have shown, more often than not there are much more mundane and pragmatic reasons behind a leader's motivations and incentives, such as self-preservation. The majority of the leadership types adopt the normative approach that leadership is a positive phenomenon generating change for the greater good. This, however, as the previous chapters have shown, is just not always true. A selfless leadership is not always pragmatic. With asymmetric leadership the realities of leadership do not always match the expectations for ideal leaders.

In asymmetric leadership in transitional processes, the inequality of the relationships and the volatility of the situation leaders appear to be particularly adept at adjusting and adapting their leadership styles to suit the situation. Adaptability, as we saw, can be achieved successfully by having high levels of self-awareness, but it may also be down to self-preservation and the need for the leadership to survive. Hence asymmetric leadership could also be characterized as survivalist leadership and its focus can be more short-term and result-based rather than long-term and inspiration-based.

In light of the unpredictable and always changing nature of asymmetric and survivalist leadership, understandably, multiple challenges arise for those who have to face and deal with such types of leadership. Empirically, in protracted conflicts, more pragmatic processes with mutually beneficial outcomes have led to successful transitions to stability and peace. In sum, the book has underlined the extent of versatility required of effective leaders in terms of style and approach.

BIBLIOGRAPHY

Azzam, Roger J, *Liban l'instruction d'un crime : 30 Ans de guerre* (Lebanon to Investigate a Crime: 30 Years of War), Cheminements (Pathways), October 1, 2005.

Abd al-Wahab ak-Kayali, *Ta'rikh Falastin al-Khdith* (*The History of Modern Palestine*), in Arabic, Beirut, Lebanon, 1985.

AbuKhalil, A., Hafez Al-Assad in 1976, available from *english. al-akhbar.com/node/8733.*

Adair J. *Action-Centred Leadership Model*, Victoria, UK: Gower Publishing, 1979.

_____. *Great Leaders*, Guildford, UK: the Talbot Adair Press, 1989.

_____. *Leadership Skills*, London, UK: IPD, 1997.

_____. *Training for Leadership*, London, UK: Macdonald and Co, 1970.

Ajami, F., *The Vanished Imam: Musa al Sadr and the Shia of Lebanon*, Ithaca, NY: Cornell University Press, 1987.

Anderson, B. *Imagined Communities*, New York: Verso, 1991.

Antonakis. J., A. Gianciolo, R. Sterberg, *The Nature of Leadership*, London, UK: Sage Publishing, 2004.

Barker, C., Alan Johnson, and Michael Lavalette, eds., *Leadership and Social Movements*, Manchester, UK: Manchester University Press, 2001.

Barr, J., *A Line in the Sand: The Anglo-French Struggle for the Middle East, 1914-1948*, New York: Norton & Company, 2013.

Bass, B. and P. Steidlmeier, "Ethics, Character and Authentic Transformational Leadership Behaviour," *Leadership Quarterly*, Vol. 10, No. 2, 1999, pp. 181-217.

Bass, B. M., *A New Paradigm of Leadership: an inquiry into Transformational Leadership*, Washington, DC: U.S. Army Institute of the Behavioural and Social Sciences, 1996.

Bauman, Z., *Postmodern Ethics*, Oxford, UK: Blackwell, 1993.

Ben-Ami, S., *A Front Without a Rearguard: A Voyage to the Boundaries of the Peace Process*, in Hebrew., Tel Aviv, Israel: Miskal-Yedioth Ahronoth Books and Chemed Books, 2004.

Blondel, J., *Political Leadership: Towards a General Analysis*, London, UK: Sage Publications, 1987.

Bowditch, J. L., and A. F. Buono, *A Primer on Organisational Behaviour*, New York: John Wiley & Sons, 1994.

Breslauer, G., *Gorbachev and Yeltsin as Leaders*, New York: Cambridge University Press, 2002.

Carlebach, E., *Anglo-American Committee of Inquiry on Jewish Problems in Palestine and Europe* [in Hebrew], Tel Aviv, Israel: Leinman, 1946, Vol. 2, p. 352.

Carlyle, T., *On Heroes, Hero Worship and the Heroic in History*, London, UK: Echo Library, 2007.

Chehabi, H. E., Houchang Chehabi, eds., *Distant Relations: Iran and Lebanon in the Last 500 Years*, London, UK: I. B. Tauris, 2007.

Chen, C. C., and Y. T. Lee, *Leadership and Management in China*, Cambridge, UK: Cambridge University Press, 2008.

Clinton, B., *My Life*, New York: Alfred A. Knopf, 2004.

Day, D., and J. Antonakis, *The Nature of Leadership*, Los Angeles, CA: Sage Publications, 2012.

Deeb, M., *Syria's Terrorist War on Lebanon and the Peace Process*, London, UK: Palgrave/Macmillan, 2003.

Douglas, M., *Natural Symbols*, London, UK: Routledge, 2003.

_____., *Purity and Danger*, London, UK: Routledge, 2008.

Durkheim, É., *De la division du travail social (The Division of Labour in Society)*, French Ed., Charleston, SC: Nabu Press, 2011.

Eban, A., *The New Diplomacy: International Affairs in the Modern Age*, Winter 1983-84.

Elpeleg, Z., David Harvey, trans., *The Grand Mufti: Haj Amin al-Hussaini, Founder of the Palestinian National Movement*, London, UK: Frank Cass, 1993.

Etzioni, A., *Modern Organisations*, London, UK: Prentice Hall, 1964.

Fayyad, S., "Why I'm Building Palestine," *Foreign Policy*, Vol. 183, December 2010.

Fiedler, F. E., *A Theory of Leadership Effectiveness*, New York: McGraw-Hill, 1967.

Forster, L., "Coalition Leadership Imperatives," *Military Review*, November-December 2000, pp. 55-60.

Freedman, L., *Transformation of Strategic Affairs*, London, UK: International Institute for Strategic Studies, 2006.

Freedman, L. and Jeffrey H. Michaels, eds., *Scripting Middle East Leaders: The Impact of Leadership Perceptions on US and UK Foreign Policy*, London, UK: Bloomsbury, 2013.

Funnel, R. G., *Leadership – Theory and Practice*, Seares House Papers, 1981.

Gabbay, R. E., *A Political Study of the Arab-Jewish Conflict: The Arab Refugee Problem, A Case Study*, Geneva, Switzerland, and Paris, France: E. Droz, 1959.

Galtung, J., *Peace by Peaceful Means: Peace and Conflict, Development and Civilization*, Oslo, Norway: PRIO, 1996.

Gayle, A. C., *Understanding Leadership*, London, UK: Sage Publications, 2004.

Gensicke, K., Alexander Fraser Gunn, trans., *The Mufti of Jerusalem and the Nazis: The Berlin Years*, London, UK: Vallentine Mitchell, 2011.

Glad, B., "Passing the Baton: Transformational Political Leadership from Gorbachev to Yeltsin; from de Klerk to Mandela," *Political Psychology*, Vol. 17, No. 1, 1996., pp. 1-28.

Goleman, D., "Leadership that Gets Results," *Harvard Business Review*, March-April 2000, pp. 78-90.

Goodarzi, J. M., *Syria and Iran: Diplomatic Alliance and Power Politics in the Middle East*, London, UK: I. B. Tauris, 2009.

Greenleaf, R., *Servant Leadership: A Journey into the Nature of Legitimate Power and Greatness*, Mahwah, NJ: Paulist Press, 2002.

Greenwald, G., *Leadership and Followership*, Chap. 9, London, UK: Sage Publications, 2007.

Grint, K., *Leadership: Limits and Possibilities*, London, UK: Palgrave/Macmillan, 2005.

Hanna, E., "Lessons Learned from the Recent War in Lebanon," *Military Review*, Vol. 87, No. 5.

_____., Unpublished paper for the writer presented to the Center of Future Strategic Studies in Cairo, Egypt, 2006.

Harari, O., *The Leadership Secrets of Colin Powell*, New York: McGraw-Hill, 2002.

Harter, N., F. J. Ziolkowski, and S. Wyatt, "Leadership and Inequality," *Leadership*, Vol. 2, No. 3, 2006, pp. 75-94.

Haslam, A, ed., *The New Psychology of Leadership: Identity, Influence and Power*, New York: Psychology Press, 2011.

Hersey, P., K. H. Blanchard, *The Management of Organisational Behaviour*, Upper Saddle River, NJ: Prentice Hall, 1977.

Hersey, P., *The Situational Leader*, Escondido, CA: Centre for Leadership Studies, 2004.

Horn, B., and Allister MacIntyre, eds., *In Pursuit of Excellence: International Perspectives of Military Leadership*, Winnipeg, Canada: Canadian Defence Academy Press, 2006.

Hourani, A., "Arab Refugees and the Future of Israel," *BBC*, as brought by *Haaretz* daily Newspaper, in Hebrew, December 1, 1949.

House, R. J., "A Path-Goal Theory of Leader Effectiveness," *Administrative Science Quarterly*, Vol. 16, 1971, pp. 321-338.

Huntington, S., *Third Wave: Democratization in the Late Twentieth Century*, Norman, OK: University of Oklahoma Press, 1993.

Kant, I., "Idea of a Universal History on a Cosmo-Political Plan," *The London Magazine*, pp. 385-393.

Karsh, E., *Fabricating Israeli History: The 'New Historians'*, London, UK: F .Cass, 1997.

Kellerman, B., "Leadership as a Political Act," B. Kellerman, ed., *Leadership: Multidisciplinary Perspectives*, Upper Saddle River, NJ: Prentice Hall, pp. 63- 89.

Khalidi, R., *Palestinian Identity: The Construction of Modern National Consciousness*, New York: Columbia University Press, 1997.

Kierkegaard, S., Papers and Journals: selection, London, UK: Penguin Books, 1996.

Kotter J. P., "Leading Change," *Harvard Business Review Press*, 2012, from Peter Northouse, *Theory and Practice*, Thousand Oaks, CA: Sage Publications, 2010.

_____., *Leading Change*, Boston, MA: Harvard Business School Press, 1996.

Kroeger, O., J. M. Thuesen, and H. Rutledge, *Type Talk at Work*, New York: Dell Publishing, 2002.

Laurence, J. P., ed., *The Peter Principle: Why Things Always Go Wrong*, New York: HarperCollins Publisher, 2009.

Lavie, E., "Intelligence Activity in the Palestinian Arena — A Critical Assessment," in Hebrew., *Mabat Malam,* a journal for intelligence and security affairs of the Israel Heritage & Commemoration Center (IICC), No. 52, December 2008.

Lederach, J. P., *The Moral Imagination: The Art and Soul of Building Peace*, Oxford, UK: Oxford University Press, 2005.

Lijphart, A., "Consociational Democracy," *World Politics*, Vol. 21, No. 2, January 1969, pp. 207-225.

Lipman-Blumen, J., *The Allure of Toxic Leaders: Why We Follow Destructive Bosses and Corrupt Politicians — And How We Can Survive Them*, Oxford, UK: Oxford University Press, 2005.

MacGregor Burns, J., *Leadership*, New York: Harper and Row, 1978.

Machiavelli, N., *The Prince*, Penguin Classics, New York: Penguin Books, 1961.

Matthews, G., I. J. Deary, M. C. Whiteman, *Personality Traits*, 2nd Ed., Cambridge, UK: Cambridge University Press, 2003.

McFaul, M., 'The Fourth Wave of Democracy and Dictatorship: Noncompetitive Transitions in the Post-Communist World," *World Politics*, 2002a, Vol. 54, No. 2, pp. 212-244.

Metcalf, H. C., *Scientific Foundations of Business Administration*, Baltimore, MD: Williams & Wilkins, 1926.

Mnassa, C., Elias Hraoui, *Awdat Al Joumhouriat min al dou-wailat ila al dawla* (*The Return of the Republic from the Statelets to the Nation-State*), Beiruit, Lebanon: Dar Annahar, 2002.

Mommsen, W. J., *The Political and Social Theory of Max Weber: Collected Essays*, Chicago, IL: University of Chicago Press, 1992.

Morris, B., *The Birth of the Palestinian Refugee Problem Revisited,* 2nd Ed., Cambridge, UK: Cambridge University Press, 2004.

_____. *Righteous Victims: A History of the Zionist-Arab Conflict, 1881-2001*, New York: Vintage, 2001.

Nassif, N., Al Riasaa Al Lubbnaniah fi Mahab al Reeh (The Lebanese Presidency in the Windward), Beiruit, Lebanon: Issam Fares Center for the Lebanese Affairs, 2007.

Northouse, P., *Leadership-Theory and Practice,* Thousand Oaks, CA: Sage Publications, 2010.

O'Brien, T., "The Role of the Transitional Leader: A Comparative Analysis of Adolfo Suarez and Boris Yeltsin," *Leadership*, Vol. 3, No. 4, pp. 419-432.

Osland, J., S. Taylor, and M. Mendenhall, "Global Leadership: Progress and Challenges," R. Bhagar and R. Steers, eds., *Cambridge Handbook of Culture, Organisations, and Work*, Cambridge, UK: Cambridge University Press, 2010, pp. 245-270.

Pasquino, G., "Political Leadership in Southern Europe: Research Problems," *West European Politics*, Vol. 13, No. 4, 1990, pp. 118-130.

Peters, T., and R. H. Waterman, *In Search of Excellence*, New York: Random House, 1982.

Plato, Πολιτεία *(Republic),* Athens, Greece: ΕΣΤΙΑ, 2007.

Popper, K., *The Logic of Scientific Discovery*, London, UK: Routledge, 1959.

Posen, B., *Sources of Military Doctrine: France, Britain and Germany between the World Wars*, Ithaca, NY: Cornell University Press, 1984, pp. 34-80.

Price, T. L., "The Ethics of Authentic Transformational Leadership," *Leadership Quarterly*, Vol. 14, No. 1, 2003, pp. 67-81.

Pundak, R., "From Oslo to Taba: What Went Wrong?" *Survival*, Vol. 43, No. 3, Autumn 2001.

Reardin, V. L., "Predicting Leadership Behaviours from Personality as Measured by the Myers-Briggs Type Indicator," Dissertation, North Carolina State University, Raleigh, NC, 1996.

Rejai, M. and Phillips Kay, *Leaders and Leadership: An Appraisal of Theory and Research*, Westport, CT: Praeger Publishers, 1997.

Renshon, S. A., "Political Leadership as Social Capital: Governing in a Divided National Culture." *Political Psychology*, Vol. 21, No. 1, 2000.

Rice, C., *No Higher Honor: A Memoir of my Years in Washington*, New York: Broadway Paperbacks, 2011.

Ronen, Y., *The Forgotten Leader: A Biography of Ahmad Al-Shuqayri* [in Hebrew], a Ph.D. Thesis, Bar-Ilan University, Ramat-Gan, Israel, 2010.

Rosen, S., "Thinking about Military Innovation," *Winning the Next War: Innovation and the Next Military*, Ithaca, NY: Cornell University Press, 1995.

Ross, D., *The Missing Peace: The Inside Story of the Fight for Middle East Peace*, New York: Farrar, Straus and Giroux, 2004.

Rubinstein, D., Dan Leon, trans., *The Mystery of Arafat*, South Royalton, VT: Steerforth Press, 1995.

Sahliyeh, E., *In Search of Leadership: West Bank Politics since 1967*, Washington, DC: The Brookings Institution, 1988.

Sheffer, G., "Moshe Sharett: The Legacy of an Innovative Moderate Leader," Gabriel Sheffer, ed., *Innovative Leaders in International Politics*, Albany, NY: State University of New York Press, 1993.

Shlaim, A., *Collusion across the Jordan: King Abdullah, the Zionist Movement, and the Partition of Palestine*, Oxford, NY: Columbia University Press, 1988.

Smith, J. A., and R. J. Foti, "A Pattern Approach to the Study of Leader Emergence," *The Leadership Quarterly*, Vol. 9, 1998, pp. 147-160.

Stogdill, R. M, *Handbook of Leadership: A Survey of the Literature*, New York, Free Press, 1974.

Sun Tzu, *The Art of War*, Nine Grounds, UK: Capstone Publishing, 2010.

Sun Tzu, *The Art of War*, Book 3, "Attack by Stratagem," available from *suntzusaid.com/book/3*.

Tajfel, H., J. C. Turner, "An Integrative Theory of intergroup Conflict," W. G. Austin and S. Worchel, eds., *The Social Psychology of Intergroup Relations*, Monterey, CA: Brooks/Cole, 1979, pp. 33-47.

Taleb, N. N., What is a "Black Swan?" Available from *www.youtube.com/watch?v=BDbuJtAiABA*.

Tannenbaum, R., and W. H. Schmidt, "How to Choose a Leadership Pattern," *Harvard Business Review*, May-June 1973, pp. 162-175, reprint of the original HBR article of March-April 1958.

Terriff, T., "Innovate or Die: Organisational Culture and the Origins of Maneuver Warfare in the United States Marine Corps," *Journal of Strategic Studies*, Vol. 29, No. 3, June 2006.

Toeffler, A., *The Third Wave*, Bantam, NY: May 1, 1984.

Tsui, A. S. Nifadkar, and A. Ou, 2007, "Cross-National Cross-Cultural Organisational Behaviour Research," *Journal of Management*, Vol. 33, No. 3, pp. 462-468.

Tucker, R. C., *Politics as Leadership*, Columbia, MO: University of Missouri Press, 1981.

von Clausewitz, Carl, M. M. Howard, ed., *On War*, Princeton, NJ: Princeton University Press, 1984.

Weber, M., "Types of Authority," Barbara Kellerman, ed., *Political Leadership: A Source Book*, Pittsburgh, PA: University of Pittsburgh Press, 1986, pp. 232-244.

Weber, M., *Economy and Society*, Berkeley, CA: University of California Press, 1978.

Yardley, I., and N. Derrick, "Understanding the Leadership and Culture Dynamic within a Military Context: Applying Theory to an Organisational and Business Context," *Defense Studies*, Vol. 7, No. 1, March 2007, pp. 21-41.

Yukl, G., *Leadership in Organisations*, Upper Saddle River, NJ: Prentice Hall, 2006.

_____., *Leadership in Organisations*, Westford, CT: Pearson Education Ltd, 2013.

Zaccaro, S. J., "Trait-Based Perspectives of Leadership," *American Psychologist*, Vol. 62, No. 1, January 2007, pp. 6-16.

Zartman, I. W., *Peacemaking in International Conflict: Methods and Techniques*, Washington, DC: United States Institute of Peace, 2007.

Internet Sources.

12 members: four Maronite, three Druses, two Greek Orthodox, one Catholic, one Shia.

150,000 refugees came to Lebanon approximately, available from *www.lgic.org/en/history_lebanon1943.php*.

An op-ed written by Ahmad Al Jarallah in the Kuwaiti newspaper, *Alsiyasa*, available from *www.aramaic-dem.org/Arabic/Archev/AL_Seyassah/37.htm*.

Asaad, H. Speech, available from *www.youtube.com/watch?v=bdckwk_bNgY*.

Brown, M. E., 'Ethnic and Internal Conflicts: Causes and Implications' in Crocker, Osler Hampson, and Aall, eds., Turbulent Peace: The Challenges of Managing International Conflict.

Cagaptay, S., and Tyler Evans, "Balancing Iran," *The American Interest Magazine*, September-October 2013, available from *www.the-american-interest.com/article.cfm?piece=1469*.

Caplan, B., *Social Intelligence: The Wisdom of Muawiya*, available from *econlog.econlib.org/archives/2012/11/social_intellig.html*.

Colombani, Jean-Marie, *Nous sommes tous Américains (We Are All Americans)*, available from *www.lemonde.fr/idees/article/2007/05/23/nous-sommes-tous-americains_913706_3232.html*.

Declaration of the Maronite Bishops, September 20, 2000, available from *www.oocities.org/capitolhill/parliament/2587/declaration.html*.

Eisenhower Doctrine, January 5, 1957, in the Cold War period after World War II, U.S. foreign policy pronouncement by President Dwight D. Eisenhower promising military or economic aid to any Middle Eastern country needing help in resisting communist aggression, available from *www.britannica.com/EBchecked/topic/181513/Eisenhower-Doctrine*.

El-Khazen, F., "Permanent Settlement of Palestinians in Lebanon: A Recipe for Conflict," *Journal of Refugee Studies*, Vol. 10, No. 3, 1997, available from *almashriq.hiof.no/ddc/projects/pspa/khazen. html*.

Flint, C., *Understanding Geopolitics*, available from *www.exploringgeopolitics.org/Interview_Flint_Colin_Structure_Agency_Identity_Peace_Networks_Geopolitical_Codes_Visions_Agents_Actors_Representations_Practices_Spaces_Powers_Environmental_Geopolitics. html*.

Haass, R. N., *The Age of Nonpolarity, What Will Follow U.S. Dominance*, available from *www.foreignaffairs.com/articles/63397/ richard-n-haass/the-age-of-nonpolarity*.

Harris, W., "Twilight Lebanon, 1990-2011," *Middle East Review of International Affairs*, Vol. 17, No. 1, Spring 2013, available from *www.gloria-center.org/2013/03/twilight-lebanon-1990-2011/*.

Hass, A., "Haniyeh: Hamas Willing to Accept Palestinian State with 1967 Borders," *Haaretz*, November 9, 2008, available from *www.haaretz.com/news/haniyeh-hamas-willing-to-accept-palestinian-state-with-1967-borders-1.256915*.

Hassan M. Fattah, *Arab League Criticizes Hezbollah for Attacks*, available from *www.nytimes.com/2006/07/17/world/africa/17iht-arabs.2224812.html?_r=0*.

Hezbollah has built its own network of communication parallel to the state's one; full secrecy and maximum operational security is wanted for the war against Israel, available from *arabic. people.com.cn/31662/6405199.html*.

History of Lebanon, Switzerland of the East, 1943 AD-1969 AD, available from *www.lgic.org/en/history_lebanon1943.php*.

Lebanese National Pact, available from *www.britannica.com/ EBchecked/topic/1380862/Lebanese-National-Pact*.

Maps of War, available from *mapsofwar.com/ind/imperial-history.html*.

The Road to a Special Regime in Mount Lebanon, available from *publishing.cdlib.org/ucpressebooks/view?docId=ft6199p06t&chunk. id=d0e1095&toc.id=&brand=ucpress*.

In 2010, the remittances to Lebanon amounted to U.S.$8,406 million, available from *www.migrationinformation.org/datahub/ remittances/Lebanon.pdf*.

Issacharoff, A., "The Hope, the Fear and the Accusations: The Peace Agreement that Remained on the Napkin," *Walla*, May 24, 2013, available from *news.walla.co.il/?w=//2644736*.

Krauthammer, C., *The Unipolar Moment*, available from *www. foreignaffairs.com/articles/46271/charles-krauthammer/the-unipolar-moment*.

Lebanon—The Riyadh Conference and the Arab Deterrent Force, available from *www.mongabay.com/history/lebanon/lebanon-the_riyadh_conference_and_the_arab_deterrent_force.html*.

Mansour, A., *Al Inquilad Ala al Taef (The Coup D'Etat on the Taef Agreement)*, Al Kandara District, Saudi Arabia: Dar Al Jadid, 1993.

Mason, D. T., *Sustaining The Peace After Civil War*, pp. 45, available from *www.strategicstudiesinstitute.army.mil/pubs/display. cfm?pubID=819*.

Matthew Levitt and Aaron Y. Zelin, *Hizb Allah's Gambit in Syria*, August 27, 2013, available from, *www.ctc.usma.edu/posts/ hizb-allahs-gambit-in-syria*.

Nasrallah, S. H, speech at the divine victory rally held in Beirut, Lebanon, available from *english.alahednews.com.lb/essaydetailsf. php?eid=709&fid=11*.

_____., May 7 speech, available from *www.youtube. com/watch?v=aSGQm1AGfgI*.

_____., speech, available from *www.youtube.com/ watch?v=xymr7fZQ__E*.

_____., "We wouldn't have snatched soldiers if we thought it would spark war," available from *www.haaretz.com/news/nasrallah-we-wouldn-t-have-snatched-soldiers-if-we-thought-it-would-spark-war-1.199556.*

Netanyahu's address in Bar-Ilan University, Israel, June 14, 2009, available from *mfa.gov.il/MFA/PressRoom/2009/Pages/Address_PM_Netanyahu_Bar-Ilan_University_14-Jun-2009.aspx.*

Patrick Seale, *The Struggle for Syria*, New Haven, CT: Yale University Press, September 10, 1987, especially the Forward of Albert Hourani.

Permanent Observer of the League of Arab States to the United Nations addressed to the President of the Security Council, available from *www.securitycouncilreport.org/atf/cf/%7B65BFCF9B-6D27-4E9C-8CD3-CF6E4FF96FF9%7D/Lebanon%20S2008392.pdf.*

R. Bolden, "What is Leadership Development: Purpose and Practice?" *Leadership South West Research Report*, Binghamton, UK: Centre for Leadership Studies, 2005, available from *business-school.exeter.ac.uk/research/areas/centres/cls/research/publications/abstract/index.php?id=66.*

Resolution 1559, 2004, available from *www.un.org/News/Press/docs/2004/sc8181.doc.htm.*

Riad Kobaissi, "From Michel Chiha to Rafik Hariri: Continuity and Discontinuity in the Process of 'Lebanoniztion'," available from *https://ecommons.lau.edu.lb:8443/xmlui/bitstream/handle/10725/1155/Riad_Kobaissi_Thesis.pdf?sequence=1.*

R. Marion and Mary Uhl-Bien, "Leadership in Complex Organizations," *The Leadership Quarterly*, Vol. 12, 2001, p. 407, available from *www.sciencedirect.com/science/journal/10489843/12.*

Saad E. I., "The 'New Middle East' Bush Is Resisting," *The Washington Post*, August 23, 2006, available from *www.washingtonpost.com/wp-dyn/content/article/2006/08/22/AR2006082200978_pf.html.*

Salibi, K., *The Modern History of Lebanon*, New York: Praeger Publications, September 30, 1976.

Schumpeter, J., *Capitalism, Socialism and Democracy*, London, UK: Routledge, 1976.

Sfeir, T., "Nasrallah hails May 7 as 'glorious day' for Resistance," *Daily Star*, available from *www.dailystar.com.lb/News/Politics/May/16/Nasrallah-hails-May-7-as-glorious-day-for-Resistance.ashx#axzz2e8Bq6u4h.*

Steinberg, M., *Kissinger Plan for Lebanon: Death by Democracy*, available from *www.larouchepub.com/eiw/public/2005/2005_20-29/2005_20-29/2005-21/pdf/41-42_21_int.pdf.*

Special Tribunal for Lebanon, UNSCR 1757, available from *www.stl-tsl.org/en/.*

The 3 'No's of Khartoum, available from *www.sixdaywar.org/content/khartoum.asp.*

"The Former French Foreign Minister Tagged USA after the Fall of USSR as a Hyper-power," *The New York Times*, available from *www.nytimes.com/1999/02/05/news/05iht-france.t_0.html?pagewanted=print.*

Totten, M. J., "Contentions, No Peace without Syria," *Commentary Magazine*, available from *www.commentarymagazine.com/2009/08/31/no-peace-without-syria/.*

What is *Wilayat al-Faqih*? available from *www.al-islam.org/shiapoliticalthought/3.htm.*

What was the 1969 Cairo Agreement between Lebanon and the PLO? available from *www.palestinefacts.org/pf_1967to1991_lebanon_cairo_1969.php.*

ENDNOTES - CHAPTER 7

1. D. Welch Larson, "Trust and Missed Opportunities in International Relations," *Political Psychology*, Vol. 18, No. 3, September 1997, p. 701.

2. Christopher Lasch, *The Culture of Narcissism*, New York: Norton, 1978.

3. J. Mann, *Rise of the Vulcans: The History of Bush's War Cabinet*, New York: Penguin Books, 2004, pp. 327.

4. K. Dalacoura, "US Democracy Promotion in the Arab Middle East since 11 September 2001: A Critique," *International Affairs*, Vol. 81, No. 5, 2005, pp. 963-979, especially p. 978.

5. Colin Gray, *Another Bloody Century: Future Warfare*, London, UK: Phoenix, 2006, p. 351.

6. J. Esposito and J. Voll, *Islam and Democracy*, New York: Oxford University Press, 1996, p. 196.

7. Terry Eagleton, *The Ideology of the Aesthetic*, Oxford, UK: Basil Blackwell, 1990, p. 24.

8. F. D. Schmitz, *Thank God They are on Our Side: The United States and Right-Wing Dictatorships 1921-1965*, Chapel Hill, NC: University of North Carolina Press, 1999; F. D. Schmitz, *The United States and Right-wing Dictatorships, 1965-1989*, Cambridge, CT: Cambridge University Press, 2006.

9. Ronen Bergman, "Lessons on Egypt from Carter and the Shah," *The Wall Street Journal*, February 1, 2011.

10. R. S. Weisman, "Rice Admits US Underestimated Hamas Strength," *The New York Times*, January 30, 2006.

11. J. Nye, *The Future of Power*, New York: Public Affairs, 2011, p. 8.

12. Francis Fukuyama, *After the Neocons: America at the Crossroads*, London, UK: Profile Books, 2006, p. 3.

ABOUT THE CONTRIBUTORS

ANASTASIA FILIPPIDOU is a lecturer at the Centre for International Security and Resilience at Cranfield University, United Kingdom (UK). Prior to her employment at Cranfield University, she was a Lecturer at the Defence Studies Department KCL, Brunel University, and she was a teaching fellow at the War Studies Department. Dr. Filippidou worked with the Centre for Defence Studies, delivering courses on terrorism and counterterrorism for the Home Office. Her research and teaching focuses on strategy and conflict resolution; psychology of war and peace; and the role of leadership in ending terrorist campaigns. Dr. Filippidou holds a B.A. (Hons); PgCert; and a Ph.D. from the Department of War Studies, King's College London, UK.

ELIAS HANNA is a retired Lebanese Army General, who has participated in training courses in military academies in Europe as well as in the United States. His main interests include geopolitical and security issues concerning the Middle East. General (Ret.) Hanna currently teaches geopolitics and causes of war at the American University of Beirut and Notre Dame University. He also has a weekly geopolitical television show on the Lebanese MTV- General View.

EYAL PASCOVICH is an adjunct lecturer at the Departments of Political Sciences at the University of Haifa and Tel Aviv University in Israel. Formerly, he was an analyst officer in the Israel Defense Forces' military intelligence and the Israeli Counter Terrorism Bureau, as well as an advisor to the Israeli Prime Minister's Office.